T0314147

PAULINE LEONARD
RACHEL J. WILDE

GETTING IN AND GETTING ON IN THE YOUTH LABOUR MARKET

Governing Young People's Employability
in Regional Context

BRISTOL
UNIVERSITY
PRESS

First published in Great Britain in 2019 by

Bristol University Press
University of Bristol
1-9 Old Park Hill
Bristol
BS2 8BB
UK
t: +44 (0)117 954 5940
www.bristoluniversitypress.co.uk

North America office:
Bristol University Press
c/o The University of Chicago Press
1427 East 60th Street
Chicago, IL 60637, USA
t: +1 773 702 7700
f: +1 773 702 9756
sales@press.uchicago.edu
www.press.uchicago.edu

British Library Cataloguing in Publication Data
A catalogue record for this book is available from the British Library.

Library of Congress Cataloging-in-Publication Data
A catalog record for this book has been requested.

ISBN 978-1-5292-0229-8 (hardback)
ISBN 978-1-5292-0231-1 (ePub)
ISBN 978-1-5292-0230-4 (ePDF)

Cover design by blu inc, Bristol
Front cover: image kindly supplied by Stocksy
Printed and bound in Great Britain by CPI Group (UK) Ltd, Croydon, CR0 4YY
Bristol University Press uses environmentally responsible print partners

To my very dear sister, Judy Baxter, who is so greatly missed. And to Audrey and Jeanne.

Contents

Acknowledgements   vi

one   Introduction: Getting In and Getting On   1
         in the UK's Youth Labour Market

two   Employability in the North East   29

three   Enterprise on the South Coast   55

four   Internships in London   83

five   Volunteering in Glasgow, Scotland   111

six   Conclusion: Inequality, Liminality and Risk   139

References   159

Index   187

Acknowledgements

We gratefully acknowledge support from the LLAKES Centre for Research on Learning and Life Chances, funded by the Economic and Social Research Council (ESRC) and based at UCL Institute of Education, for the project entitled Getting In and Getting On in the Youth Labour Market: Entry Practices, Under-employment and Skill Formation in Regional Economies. We would particularly like to acknowledge colleagues in Theme One: Youth, Intergenerational Mobility and Civic Values – LLAKES Centre Director Andy Green, Bryony Hoskins, Michaela Franceschelli, Germ Janmaat and Avril Keating. Emily Rainsford at the University of Newcastle provided much appreciated additional inspiration and support. We would also like to thank the reviewers of the book, especially for the revisions where the knowledge and wisdom demonstrated was very much appreciated.

Our greatest debt is to all the participants in our research, many of whom went out of their way to provide us with time, advice and thoughts. We have tried our best to do justice to their experiences, insights and passion in this book.

ONE

Introduction: Getting In and Getting On in the UK's Youth Labour Market

> Young people today are more streetwise than my generation, they've been to more places, seen more things, their view of life is very streetwise. What's lacking is those skills you need to be able to work with people effectively – working as a team, self-confidence, self-discipline. We think young people are leaving school unprepared for the fact that the world of work is a very different environment to school. (John Cridland, CBI Director, cited in Crossley, 2014)

That today's young people lack necessary employability skills and are insufficiently 'job ready' on leaving education has been a dominant political discourse within Western societies for nearly 50 years. The fact that, in this context, many young people have almost routinely faced challenges in accessing good-quality work and careers of choice over this period has been a topic of high concern for governments, employers, academic researchers, media and families alike. The 2008–12 economic recession deepened anxieties still further, as youth unemployment spiralled across Europe, reaching 21 per cent in the UK, compared with 8 per cent across the labour market as a whole (Francis-Devine, 2015). Together, these institutions have systematically tended to conceptualize the problem as an individualistic issue, a 'supply-side fundamentalism' (Peck and Theodore, 2000) that positions young people – and their insufficient capabilities – at the heart of the matter. Perceived as damaging for a competitive and sustainable economy, a key activation within the UK, as in other neoliberal economies, has been to invest in bespoke training schemes to enhance young people's workplace-specific skills. Across the diverse regions of the UK, as well as across the spectrum of industrial and occupational sectors, a broad range of work 'entry route' schemes has burgeoned for young people of all social and educational backgrounds.

The starting point for this book is to explore what it is like for young people to undergo employability training as a pathway into work in the UK. Recognizing that this is a wide-ranging and somewhat 'baggy' category, and that young people's employment opportunities vary significantly across the regions of the UK (EY Foundation, 2016), we look at four different schemes in order to capture some of the diversity encompassed: employability skills in the North East; enterprise on the South Coast; internships in London; and volunteering in Glasgow, Scotland. Drawing on new and original ethnographic case study research conducted as part of the LLAKES Centre for Research on Learning and Life Chances funded by the Economic and Social Research Council, we reveal how the aims and objectives of such schemes are often a challenge to meet. These aims are to facilitate young people, often with vastly varying circumstances, not only to enter work, but, hopefully, to find jobs and careers that are meaningful, supportive, sustainable *and* enjoyable. However, such aims are often set against a regional context of constrained economic and labour market opportunities for young people. As well as exploring the perspectives of young people on the programmes themselves, a second purpose of the book therefore is to include the voices, strategies and motivations of local policy makers and training providers, whose mission it is to achieve employability skills development in their regional context. The variety of the schemes we include demonstrates how social inequality is a critical challenge, such that social class and educational background continue to play a significant role in the outcomes young people achieve. At the same time, the global contextual background of persistent economic fluctuations and changing skills needs continues to disrupt the smoothness of youth transitions from education to work for *all* young people.

A third aim of the book is to contribute theoretically to our understanding of the 'why' and 'how' of policy on youth employability training in the UK context. Through the theoretical lens of a post-Foucauldian governmentality approach (McKee, 2009), we take a dual focus on the discursive field – the space where the 'problem' is identified and policy solutions proposed – and the interventionist practices, as manifest in the organizations that design and run the specific programmes and techniques by which, in this case, young people's employability is governed. By emphasizing the connection between current and dominant thinking and policy on young people and work, and ensuing practical modes of youth governance, we demonstrate how different employability schemes planned in diverse geographical and economic regional landscapes are operationalized in practice. We show that, on the one hand, through the intersecting strategies of trainers and work experience providers, young people from diverse social and regional backgrounds may be harnessed with the resources, resilience and dispositions to secure good-quality work and economic stability, while on the other, schemes may function only to reproduce, or further entrench, social inequalities and vulnerability to ongoing liminality and risk.

For a rigorous analysis, investigation at an interconnecting range of scales is therefore needed to understand and evaluate young people's education-to-work transitions. This must include national policy discourses on young people and employment; macro-regional economic policies and geographical senses of place; micro-organizational constructions of young people; and young people themselves. As we go on to outline more fully later in this chapter, the aim of our theoretical framework is to enable us to interrogate this multi-level complexity and explain how macro-level policies are articulated through micro-level practices. This involves illuminating the importance of power and resources, and the daily expressions of these, that perpetuate inequalities across these social and spatial fields. First, however, we briefly lay out the terrain of youth transitions towards employability, in theory and policy terms.

Conceptualizing youth-to-work transitions in global and national context

The notion that 'youth' is a socially significant stage of the lifecourse, bridging childhood and adulthood and having distinct roles, has its roots in the early functionalist sociology of the first half of the 20th century (France, 2016). Within this theoretical tradition, the period of youth was conceptualized as the time when, in all types of societies, young people were taught the pathways into socially acceptable forms of adulthood and adult behaviours (Eisenstadt, 1956). This conceptualization of youth underpinned the theoretical development of the 'youth transitions' school that emerged during the 1960s and 1970s. As we discuss more fully later in this section, at a time when Western governments were beginning to roll out the neoliberal political agenda that was to mark the remainder of the century, it was becoming clear to governments and academic researchers that the once quite predictable pathways that were assumed to exist for young people were being undermined, leaving them increasingly vulnerable to the risk of 'failing' to transition. While the functionalist model on which such discourses rest was recognized and critiqued theoretically (Cohen and Ainley, 2000), perceptions of youth as a stage of potential vulnerability and risk fed into policy, with governments anxious to mitigate against the costs and lost benefits of young people's 'failed' transitions.

A primary risk factor for young people was the fact that, from the 1970s onwards, the employment landscape was beleaguered by several significant changes, both global and national in scale (McDowell, 2002; Furlong and Cartmel, 2007; Simmons et al, 2014b). New sources of competition developing within emerging nations had led to increased outsourcing of manufacturing and heavy industry within advanced economies such as the UK, generating the contracting and restructuring of many traditional, regional employment opportunities (France and Roberts, 2017). As the 20th century progressed, de-industrialization and transitions to service- and knowledge-based economies, growth in post-Fordist work practices and the hiking of the price of oil prompted a wage–price inflationary spiral in Western economies and generated more flexible and non-standard forms of employment, whereby notions of 'jobs for life' were vanishing fast. Economic performance was volatile and fluctuating, with periods of recession and rises in mass unemployment a regular feature, routinely hitting certain sections of the labour market – such as young people – the hardest. The economic decline that commenced in 2008 and started to alleviate during 2012, often dubbed the 'Great Recession' (Bell and Blanchflower, 2010), hit young people particularly deleteriously. In the UK, 74 per cent of the reduction in employment was among those aged 16–24 (Bell and Blanchflower, 2010), and while conditions were bad for all, it was far worse for those already in poverty and in declining regions (Crosnoe, 2014; Schoon, 2014; EY Foundation, 2016). Towards the end of the period, the International Labour Organization (ILO) claimed that a growing number of young people across Europe 'had given up hope of finding a job and have dropped out of the labour market altogether' (ILO, 2012: 84). The notion of a 'precariat' as a 'new dangerous class' (Standing, 2011), whose members' lives were marked by continual insecurity and transient, meaningless work, gained traction, particularly in relation to youth employment.

Thus while much academic attention has been paid to the 'Great Recession' and the supposedly 'lost generation' of the late noughties (Nilsen and Brannen, 2014), it is judicious to place these events in historical context and acknowledge the legacy of labour market transformations over the past 40–50 years (at the very least). In the UK, as Furlong and colleagues (2018) argue, whether there was *ever* a 'golden age' for young people, in which 'jobs were plentiful and unemployment short-lived' is questionable (Goodwin and O'Connor, 2005: 205). Up until the 1980s recession, manual work accounted for many of the job opportunities for young people, especially for those from working-class families who tended to leave school at the minimum age. Yet as traditional industrial occupations were dwindling in regional economies, so the availability of apprenticeships was shrinking. While rates of employment remained relatively full, fears of unemployment were ever-present, and frequent job changing marked this period, just as it does in present times (Goodwin and O'Connor, 2005). The dominance of piecework in the 1960s, '70s and '80s, whereby wages were directly related to personal productivity, meant that long hours needed to be worked in many industrial sectors in order to accumulate a liveable income. Then, as now, working life thus presented challenges to young people. Then, as now, there was a tension between 'getting in' and 'getting on': accessing good-quality, stable and sustainable careers. This was a tension patterned by social background, as more young people from middle-class than working-class backgrounds stayed on at school and progressed into higher education, thereby ensuring the qualifications and networks to provide them with entry routes into the more secure and better remunerated professional and managerial careers.

The increasingly uncertain global economic context fuelled government anxieties about the UK's relative economic decline in the global market and falling economic standards. From the late 1970s onwards, a profound and critical questioning of young people's education, skills and abilities, and the extent to which these met the needs of business and industry (Simmons et al, 2014a; Simmons, 2017), came to dominate policy agendas. In other words, for successive governments it was perceived deficits within the education system, and the 'worklessness' and personal failings of some sections of British youth, that were identified as 'the problem', thereby decoupling macro-economic concerns from consideration (Orton, 2011). As such, the solution was seen to lie in initiatives such as the expansion of higher education to widen participation and the development of 'employability skills training'.

The first specific 'employability' intervention was the Youth Opportunities Programme introduced in 1978, to be delivered primarily through local further education establishments (Simmons, 2017). This provided the legacy for a raft of employability initiatives to follow, such as Entry to Employment (2001) and, in response to the economic crisis of 2008 onwards, the UK's Young Person's Guarantee (2010) and the Work Programme (Orton, 2011; for a critical analysis, see Adkins, 2015). The UK was not alone in its concerns for the poor opportunities for young people and benefitted from the European Union's (EU) joined-up approach through the EU Youth Guarantee (EU, 2013). This began with investments of €6.4 billion to guarantee that all young people under the age of 25 receive a good-quality offer of employment, education or training, with €206 million allocated to the UK Youth Initiative in 2014–15. A further boost of around £90 million was announced by the UK government in 2018, where money lying dormant in bank accounts was to be invested to help disadvantaged young people into work (Cabinet Office, 2018). Yet while these demonstrate some significant steps forward in terms of levels of funding, what has not shifted is the assumption that unemployment and, more fundamentally, 'worklessness' are primarily individual-level behavioural and cultural shortcomings, rather than an inevitable contingency of the changing nature of global economies and unpredictable labour markets (Crisp and Powell, 2017). Core assumptions of the 'deterioration of skills, work habits and commitment among individuals over time'

(Crisp and Powell, 2017: 1788) have consistently underpinned both discourses and policies of youth employability.

A further major problem within the contemporary policy landscape is the lack of recognition that the UK's education systems produce very unequal skills outcomes and 'are doing very little, if anything, to improve the comparatively low and stalling levels of social mobility' (Green, 2017: 88). Skills inequalities contribute to wage inequalities, which in turn are associated with multiple negative social consequences. Of particular concern is that most of the inequality in skills is experienced by those young people who fail to complete secondary education, meaning there is a section of young people who are persistently the most vulnerable. While issues of intergenerational inequality affect all young people born after 1979 (Green, 2017), it is those who fail to complete secondary education who are the least likely to fare as well as their parents' generation in employment terms. This is even more exaggerated for young people in this group who were entering the labour market at the time of the 2008 financial crisis and the ensuing years of recession and austerity – a 'jilted generation' who, it is widely held, will face more limited opportunities than their parents, 'and may be the first generation to do so since those born at the start of the last century' (Green, 2017: 1).

A key legacy of employability policy initiatives, reflecting the generalizing tendency by successive governments to 'mainstream' the voluntary sector since the turn of the century (Halford et al, 2015), has been that third sector organizations (TSOs), often through local partnerships, have been increasingly targeted as deliverers of employability skills training, particularly for young people disengaged from and disaffected by formal education and training systems (Thomson and Russell, 2009; Ellis Paine et al, 2013). As we discuss in Chapter Three, concern was growing that a 'welfare dependency' was developing within this group, forming an emerging class marked by anti-social and anti-work attitudes (Standing, 2011; France and Roberts, 2017). A 'new' and different approach was needed to tackle this. Positioned as alternative in ethos and methods, TSOs were therefore encouraged to design curriculums by which individual young people's skills, attitudes and job-seeking approaches are enhanced (Thompson, 2011). In addition, and not restricted to this group, performing unpaid work or 'volunteering' is frequently posited within government policy discourses as a means by which young people should acquire valuable workplace experience, perceived as critical to both getting a job and operating effectively once in post (Newton et al, 2011; Ellis Paine et al, 2013; DirectGov, 2016; see Chapter Five). More recently, as youth labour markets were particularly squeezed during the 2008–12 economic recession, young people are increasingly being endorsed by a further political grammar: that of enterprise, a term embracing a set of moral values and 'wicked solutions' to 'think big', be 'entrepreneurial' and develop the skills to create one's own job opportunities (Wilde and Leonard, 2018; see also Chapter Three). This period also witnessed a burgeoning of internships, whereby specific professions in high demand by young people, such as the creative industries, law and finance, offered short-term 'work experience'. While, as we discuss in Chapter Four, some high-quality schemes have emerged, much was unpaid and not always productive in terms of new skills acquisitions.

It was through this developing policy context, therefore, that the concept of 'employability' came increasingly to be 'the new buzzword in labour market policy circles' (Peck and Theodore, 2000: 729). Not restricted to young people, the term encompassed both the unemployed looking for work and those in employment but seeking better jobs with either a different or their current employer (McQuaid and Lindsay, 2005; McQuaid et al, 2005). However, both in policy and academic theorizing, it has remained a contested concept, derided as, in the main, reflecting and even reinforcing the 'supply-side fundamentalism' (Peck and Theodore, 2000: 729) of policy approaches that place the responsibility for unemployment squarely at the feet of the unemployed themselves, maintaining that 'the state has neither the responsibility nor the capability to create jobs' (Peck and Theodore, 2000: 729; Crisp and Powell, 2017). From this perspective, the causes of unemployment are to be remedied through close scrutiny of the behaviour, motivations and skills of those individuals judged as 'deficient', most often those in the former industrial regions, vulnerable communities and/or those lacking in educational qualifications (Danson, 2005; HM Government, 2011; Orton, 2011; Crisp and Powell, 2017). In contrast, a broader view understands employability as incorporating, or being caused by, demand-side factors, such as the sustainable opportunities within regional labour markets and the actual prospects not only for *getting in* to relevant, good-quality work, but also for *getting on* in terms of job retention and progression (Hillage and Pollard, 1998; Devins and Hogarth, 2005; Houston, 2005; McQuaid and Lindsay, 2005; McQuaid et al, 2005; Lindsay and Houston, 2011; Adam et al, 2017). However, while there are occasional encouraging signs that the government is acknowledging the critical role of employers in youth employability (UKCES, 2013; Adam et al, 2017), academic interrogation of the concept, and the ways in which it has been deployed in youth employment policy, reveal a gradual harshening of the supply-side approach towards a more punitive regime, characterized by increasing conditionality, benefit sanctions and spending cuts (Adkins, 2015; Crisp and Powell, 2017). Rather than alleviating youth unemployment, policy, it is argued, is reinforcing a cohort of young people increasingly at risk of worklessness and poverty in relation to adult workers (MacInnes et al, 2013; Crisp and Powell, 2017). As a term that aims to capture the ability of young people to access work, 'employability' is, therefore, often value-laden with moral judgements and implied policy recommendations. Conceptualizing young people's employment capacities and prospects more holistically has thus become identified by analysts as paramount.

This need has intensified in recent years, not least due to the so-called 'Great Recession', which, as mentioned earlier, produced new representations of a generation as 'jilted' (Howker and Malik, 2010) and 'betrayed' (Ainley, 2016), let down by both policy and economics. For academic researchers, the interest is part of the broader philosophical turn to attempting to understand what is deemed to be the 'increasing' unpredictability of the post/modern world, and the assumption that:

> individuals act in a greater variety of contexts and milieus than previous generations, when these contexts and milieus are shaped more obviously than before by mostly intangible forces and when individuals thus act and think against a background of a seemingly infinite plethora of options, the way we *do* adulthood too is subject to pluralization and to interminable change. (Blatterer, 2010b: 10–11; emphasis in original)

How young people fare in this increasingly uncertain context where, it is claimed, new opportunities and choice have expanded but, consequently, risk has intensified, has been predominantly conceptualized within the broad theoretical church of 'youth transitions.' This approach not only draws on the ongoing structural changes in Western industrialized economies to explain the increasing flexibility, non-linearity and rising insecurity of lifecourse patterns, but combines these with attention to the ideological discourses underpinning neoliberalism, such as individualization, de-traditionalism and liquid modernity, which posit that, in order to cope with the uncertain milieus, ongoing, reflexive and individualized planning and negotiation is now necessary for all (Beck, 1992a; Bauman, 1999; Beck and Beck-Gernsheim, 2002). For young people, where once families and local employers played a key part in determining 'what next', the impetus is increasingly placed on them as individuals to scout for opportunities and tailor their own life trajectories (Heinz, 2009; Price et al, 2011). Increasingly untrammelled/unsupported by the normative force of social structural positions, produced through *inter alia* class, gender, race and ethnicity, religion, place and community, routes to adulthood are marked not only by augmented autonomy and flexibility, but also by multiple, fragmented and evermore 'extended' or 'delayed' transitions (Helve and Evans, 2013; Quintin and Martin, 2014). The shift from education to work may not only take longer, but it may also be non-linear, and (young) people may go backwards and forwards between the two (Worth, 2005).

While profoundly influential, these explanations have been heavily critiqued. A principal concern is that they 'mute and obscure' (Cohen and Ainley, 2000: 80) the differences between young people, depicting them as a relatively homogenous group. While economic recessions, not least the 2008–12 recession, undoubtedly had youth-wide implications, evidence consistently supports the fact that class, race and gender-based structural inequalities continue to wield a considerable differentiating influence over the lives and actions of young people (France and Roberts, 2017), especially in terms of employment opportunities. Risk, it is argued, is in itself socio-structurally differentiated, and class, in particular, 'still plays a significant role' in youth transitions into precarious labour markets (Shildrick et al, 2009: 459; Roberts, 2012; Leonard et al, 2016). Individualism remains 'bounded' by social biography, as young people negotiate the labour market and other spheres of life according to their capital and resources (Evans, 2002; Green, 2017). Class, as well as gender and race, thus not only remain integral to the prediction of origins and destinations, but are also ongoing, productive and dynamic forces over careers and the lifecourse (France and Roberts, 2017).

Research revealing the purchase of social class background on youth transitions into education and employment has predominantly tended to focus on the extreme ends of social structures: *either* on the relatively successful middle classes (for example, Tomlinson, 2007; Wilton, 2011; Tholen, 2013; Brooks, 2017) *or* on the under-privileged, worst-off sections of the working class (for example, MacDonald et al, 2005; Thomson, 2011; White and Green, 2011; Simmons et al, 2014a); and occasionally comparing the two (Tomaszewski and Cebulla, 2014). This body of research paints a powerful yet highly divided picture. On the one hand, while all graduates were undoubtedly deleteriously affected by the 2008–12 recession (Bell and Blanchflower, 2011; Hoskins et al, 2017), those from more privileged backgrounds remain more likely to gain access into elite universities and thereafter achieve higher status, better remunerated and more stable employment than those from lower-middle and working-class backgrounds (Britton et al, 2016). On the other hand, working-class young people, especially those from the most deprived areas of the UK, are less likely to enter any sort of higher education, elite or 'new', and are far more likely to be unemployed in the long term, or cycling between 'poor work', low paid and on insecure contracts (France, 2016). However, while our knowledge of the youth transitions marking the upper and lower ends of the class spectrum is improving, as Roberts (2011) notes, there remains a 'missing middle' in our knowledge about the circumstances of young people who progress to merely 'getting by' in 'ordinary' work (Roberts and MacDonald, 2013): neither 'NEET' (not in education, employment or training) nor high-flying graduates/young professionals.

Significantly intersecting with class are other social identities such as gender, race, disability, caring responsibilities and so on. The gendered nature of work and employment is well established (Halford and Leonard, 2001, Walkerdine et al, 2001), and young women, particularly those with caring responsibilities, are more likely to be, involuntarily, in low-paid, insecure, part-time and temporary work (IPPR, 2010; Brinkley et al, 2013). While young women, on the one hand, are more likely than men to attend higher education (France, 2016), they are still more heavily represented in arts, humanities and health subjects, which are less likely to lead into more highly paid careers. This occupational segregation continues in vocational education and training, where young women are more likely to be in hairdressing, social care and health (Leonard et al, 2018). This binary is complicated by race, however. While Asian and Black ethnic groups overall experience higher rates of unemployment than White young people, young Asian and Black men fare worse than women in the 16–24 age group (TUC, 2014) In 2012, it was estimated that half of young Black males were unemployed (Ball et al, 2012). While, overall, youth employment figures have since much improved, unemployment for Other ethnic groups is still double that of Whites, and Black and Asian graduates are still more than twice as likely to be unemployed (TUC, 2016; GOV.UK, 2018b). Similar rates of unemployment are experienced by young carers, who are also twice as likely to be not in education, employment or training (Carers Trust, nd). Figures are even worse for young people with a disability, who are four times more likely to be unemployed than young people without a disability (Burchardt, 2005). The challenge therefore is to gain greater understanding of the contextual factors affecting work transitions across the full complexity of youth diversity. As we outlined previously, this involves investigation of how macro–economic employment policies affect micro–institutional processes, such as labour market entry routes and employability training, for young people from a wide range of social backgrounds. In this book, we argue that this attention should also be intersected by geography: by the spaces and places of regional economies, many of which may also be merely 'getting by', dominated by, at best, 'ordinary' and, at worst, low-quality work.

Theoretical approach of the book

Our approach in this book is primarily inspired by Foucault's work on governmentality, which was concerned with tracing the historical shifts in constructions of knowledge and exercises of disciplinary power in modern societies (Elden, 2007; McKee, 2009). Foucault was particularly interested in the 'art of governing': exploring the practices and calculated strategies of government and other institutions, such as schools and prisons, and how power is exercised to make populations more 'docile', 'productive' and 'improved' (Foucault, 2003). In other words, 'this is not government with an -*ality* suffixed, but with a *govern*-prefixed. A mentality to be governed' (Dean, 2013: 46; emphasis in original). This does not imply passivity or powerlessness among citizens, however, but a system of regulatory guidance that facilitates different possibilities for action, employing a range of tactics calculated to shape, regulate and/or manage activities (Inda, 2005; Dean, 2013). This type of governance, the '"conduct of conduct", in which "conduct" means the regulation or controlling of ourselves and others' (Warburton and Smith, 2003: 772–3), is therefore intimately involved with the everyday lives and thoughts of its peoples, positioning them as 'subjects' (Foucault, 1980) through the shaping of the private self for socio-political ends.

Building on these ideas, other commentators have developed the theoretical perspective more widely, coining this as the 'post-Foucauldian governmentality approach' (McKee, 2009). This draws attention to the 'how' of governing through a focus on both:

> the *discursive field* in which the exercise of power is rationalized – that is the space in which the problem of government is identified and solutions proposed; and the actual *interventionist practices* as manifest in specific programmes and techniques in which both individuals and groups are governed according to these aforementioned rationalities. (Lemke, 2001) (McKee, 2009: 466; emphasis in original)

Post-Foucauldian governmentality is therefore fundamentally a political project that identifies and problematizes a particular social space and subsequent means of intervention. It also directs attention to the ways in which both discourses and practices transfer a *moral* dimension, often seeking to purport truths 'about who we are and who we should be' (McKee, 2009: 468; see also Rose, 1999). Such positions, or subjectivities, are never fixed or universal, but heterogeneous and historically contingent: constructions that 'represent particular responses to particular problems at particular times' (McKee, 2009: 468). In addition, and importantly, governmentality is not only done *to* subjects, but people are active in their own self-government, exercising power upon themselves. Rose (1999), for example, has noted how individuals, or 'welfare subjects', seek to shape their own subjectivities through techniques of self-improvement. As commentators working with this approach from poststructuralist and feminist perspectives have noted, this is an understanding of power as fundamentally productive, facilitative and creative, not only producing conformist, 'docile' bodies, but allowing for possibilities of individual agency and liberation, of negotiation and even contestation and resistance. Thus, although post-/ Foucauldian approaches see that 'the subject' in poststructuralism is always socially constructed within discourses, they are also 'capable of resistance and innovations produced out of the clash between contradictory subject positions and practices' (Baxter, 2003: 30).

Foucault's governmentality approach schematizes three kinds of power–knowledge that operate in a nexus: the sovereign, judicial form, which works through declaring what is to be prevented (for example, policy discourses on 'unemployable' young people); the disciplinary form, which works through specifying what must be done (for example, interventions to equip young people with 'skills'); and the security form, which involves

standing back sufficiently so that one can grasp the point at which things are taking place, whether or not they are desirable. This means trying to grasp them at the level of their nature, or ... grasping them at the level of their effective reality. (Foucault, 2007: 46–7, cited in Hodge and Harris, 2012: 161)

This approach is useful for the aims of this book, which are to explore the discursive fields of recent youth employability policy in the UK, both at national and regional levels; a range of interventions, or entry route programmes, which have been established in the attempt to better position young people to develop the skills deemed requisite for employment and the actual practices of trainers and managers involved in operationalizing these on the ground. We are inspired by how the concept of governmentality has proved productive in the analysis of similar policy contexts, such as unemployment case management (McDonald and Marston, 2005); adult learning (Nicoli and Fejes, 2008); vocational competency-based training (Hodge and Harris, 2012); youth non-participation (Fergusson, 2013); youth volunteering (Dean, 2013); and student gap years (Wilde, 2016). This work has demonstrated how governmentality provides a valuable theoretical perspective for understanding how power and rule articulate within and through policy initiatives aiming to govern young people's transitions into work and support the UK economy, as well as to become 'well-rounded citizens' and support social cohesion (Dean, 2013). In this context, governmentality remains, under Foucault's analysis, a reactive and reflexive approach, steering young people to meet economic and social aims through a range of apparatuses designed to produce and internalize a certain set of 'responsible behaviours' (Dean, 2013: 49).

A key insight is that governmentality highlights 'how emergent mentalities of rule are made both practical and technical within specific organized practices for directing human conduct' (McKee, 2009: 467). The perspective focuses first on the analysis of discourse: forms of knowledge or powerful sets of assumptions, expectations and explanations which, in the ways that they inform and frame policies, strategies, programmes and techniques at the macro-level, govern subjects and produce social practices at the micro-level (Baxter, 2003; McDonald and Marston, 2005; McKee, 2009). Significant here also, however, are the ways in which individuals are active in their *own* government and shape their own subjectivities. For example, whether designed and run by the state, private or third sector, employability training schemes, as part of the discursive apparatus of a 'workfare state' (Jessop, 2002), are dominated by liberal-humanist discourses of individualization, responsibilization and participation, which, reflecting our earlier discussion, emphasize the active engagement of individual young people (McDonald and Marston, 2005; Hodge and Harris, 2012; Fergusson, 2013). As we demonstrate through the various schemes we analyze in this book, these discourses inform both their technologies of agency, whereby trainees' capacities for participation and action are enhanced and improved, and their technologies of performance, whereby these capacities are compared and calculated so they may be optimized (McDonald and Marston, 2005). Thus, trainees are routinely expected not only to sign up for training (often as a condition of welfare) and have their competencies evaluated, but also to become accountable for their own learning, usually by grasping the opportunity to manage and appraise their own performance in various ways: 'an exemplary disciplinary apparatus' (Hodge and Harris, 2012: 158; see also Edwards and Usher, 1994). Failure to perform in this way may be constructed as a wilful authoring of one's own misfortune, thereby firmly positioning the responsibility for unemployment at the level of individuals themselves (Fergusson, 2013).

Governmentality is therefore an approach with a broad sphere of interest, exploring the exercise of political control, relations with social institutions and communities, and self-government. As a mode of analysis that lends itself to any context involving 'the deliberate regulation of human conduct towards particular ends ... highlighting how government is ubiquitous in all social relationships, even in the most mundane activities at the finest minutia' (McKee, 2009: 469), it is, therefore, highly appropriate to the mission of this book to explore and compare the entry route and labour market experiences of young people in different regional policy contexts in the UK. Here, therefore, we are investigating three levels of governance: the macro-level of the national and, as policy outcomes are the necessarily contingent consequence of the actions and interactions of *all* those involved in the process of service delivery, the meso-level of the regional and the micro-level of the organizational: those who actually deliver policies 'on the front line' (Prior and Barnes, 2011), such as trainers within employability training organizations and line managers overseeing work experience placements. It is at this level where 'the context-specific interpretations and negotiations shaped by agents' values, motivations and understandings' (Prior and Barnes, 2011: 265) will define the actual experience of policy on young people. To what extent can the different actors at the organizational level be conceptualized as 'engineers' (Rose 1999), complicit with government agendas? Or do they deploy subversive strategies to negotiate modifications and/or localized, alternative positions for and with the young trainees? Finally, but certainly no less importantly, a key concern is the exploration of how young people themselves negotiate the attempts to manage them at both regional and programme levels, and how they accept, adopt or refuse these attempts, or approach them with disinterest.

Further, building on the focus on the regional and the local, it is our theoretical intention to connect our analysis to the spaces and places within which the employability policies and social practices are produced. Our approach exposes the ways in which the experience of training is a co-production of political, historical, social, economic and cultural factors that are spatially specific to the regions in which they are based. As argued elsewhere (Leonard, 2010), space is not a neutral backdrop; it is thoroughly implicated in the construction and performance of particular social and cultural practices, identities and social relations through its materiality, its histories and cultures (Lefebvre, 1991). In line with our post-Foucauldian perspective, and drawing on Lefebvre (1991), we show, for example, that whether training happens in the North East, on the South Coast, in London or Glasgow in Scotland matters: it is through the lived dimensions of these distinctive places that opportunities, experiences, meanings and identities are co-produced.

The research

The book is based on new, original research conducted between 2014 and 2017 as part of the ESRC-funded LLAKES Centre's larger research programme exploring youth, intergenerational mobility and civic values. Within this, our research study investigated the fact that a number of 'youth labour markets' now exist in the UK, providing highly differentiated opportunities for an expanding age group of young people (aged 16–28) seeking and preparing for different forms of work. To access these opportunities, young people are competing for often limited and highly competitive places through the growing use of different forms of extended entry practices, such as employability programmes, enterprise schemes, internships and voluntary work placements across the public, private and third sectors. As discussed previously, these schemes are likely to be particularly important for young people with few educational qualifications, family resources and networks and/or living in more vulnerable communities. Our aim is to examine how young people fare across the different regions of the UK in terms of 'getting in' and 'getting on': transitioning from education into sustainable work and careers, and the extent to which strategies for regional economic growth and regeneration depend on, exacerbate or ameliorate entry route practices for young people. We were particularly concerned to investigate the impact of social class, in intersection with gender and race on employability training and good work outcomes.

The project employed mixed methods, combining policy analysis, literature review and visits, to build case studies of youth labour markets in contrasting regions of the UK. We aimed for regional economic diversity, but all the regions we selected contained working-class neighbourhoods that had, historically, been suffering from deprivation, poverty and youth unemployment, which the recession had only exacerbated. Within these, we looked for regions that had, as a consequence, implemented clear youth employment policies. We then selected case study sites where local policies had identified particular 'routes' that were distinctively connected with the region's economic geography and aimed for diversity within these, while covering the major entry route schemes. Glasgow in Scotland and the North East of England were both regions suffering from long-standing structural decline, having historically relied on manufacturing and heavy industry for local employment. However, Scotland also offered a distinctive opportunity to investigate whether, under a different government, different approaches towards youth employability were evident. Youth unemployment levels, at over 25 per cent, were similar in Glasgow and the North East, both identified as among the UK's employment 'blackspots' (in 2012) (Work Foundation, 2014).

The South Coast was selected as also having a distinctive regional economy: in this case, based on the maritime industry. Before the advent of cheap air travel, the South Coast had thrived on ship building and tourism. While their decline meant that the region also contained some of the most impoverished neighbourhoods in Europe (Brown, 2013), the diversity of industry that subsequently developed in the region meant that, compared with Scotland and the North East, youth unemployment was lower (about 13 per cent in 2012) (Work Foundation, 2014). London's highly diverse social, political and economic mix offered a further point of contrast, its high unemployment rate during the recession partially explained by the fact that it has the highest proportion of young people in higher education (EY Foundation, 2016). However, in 2012 the youth unemployment rate was comparable to that of the South Coast (Work Foundation, 2014).

All regions, including Scotland, had access to a range of funding: national and regional, as well as from the EU through the European Social Fund. Glasgow had received additional funds through its hosting of the Commonwealth Games in 2014 (as we discuss more fully in Chapter Five). All had drawn on this funding to develop specific youth employability policies to tackle their economic challenges, often concentrating on specific entry route initiatives that were seen to be relevant and hold promise for the region.

As our aim was to explore the experiences of young people from across the social structure, we thus selected a broad range of entry route schemes. As discussed in detail in the chapters that follow, our case studies focused on employability training in the North East; enterprise schemes on the South Coast; volunteering as a key strategy for young people in Glasgow; and internships in London. These were highly diverse in terms of the young people they were aimed at, spanning those with higher educational qualifications, those who had left school aged 18 with Level 2 qualifications, and those who had left school with no qualifications at all. Within each of these case study organizations, we conducted in-depth ethnographies of between one and three weeks in duration, undergoing the training alongside the young people, involving classroom-based sessions and work experience. We took extensive fieldnotes, based on our participant observation and informal chats with young people and trainers, and supplemented these with 55 semi-structured interviews with key informants: policy makers and practitioners in the field of youth employment. These varied somewhat according to region: in Glasgow and the North East, those in charge of youth employment initiatives were based within the local councils, where specific roles had been established to tackle youth employment. In addition, in Scotland, we talked to the Scottish Government, which has a specific strategy for youth employment in Scotland. On the South Coast, policy making for employment was overseen by the Local Enterprise Partnership, and so we sought out its views. However, there was no specific role responsibility for youth unemployment, and it proved quite difficult to access people to talk to us about this. In London, we talked primarily to non-government organizations aiming to support young people's employment within the capital. This diversity is interesting, revealing differences in the way that local regions position and prioritize (youth) employability within overall regional strategic policy making.

We also conducted 54 semi-structured interviews with young people aged between 16 and 28 years old. Informed by our governmentality perspective, with policy-making informants we discussed views on key local labour market challenges, policy initiatives and the rationale for these, and the future aims, and outlook for, young people in the region. With the trainers and work placement managers, we discussed programme objectives and design, skills-training approaches and the types of young people attracted to, or compulsorily allocated to, the training programme. With the young people, we took a biographical approach to exploring their educational and employment histories, their career aspirations and reasons for attending their training course, and their views on, and evaluations of, the quality of their training and work placement experiences.

Due to our ethnographic methodology, our approach to the analysis that follows is to acknowledge fully our role in the research process. To this end, we position ourselves openly within the presentation and discussion of the research, and its analysis is of course our interpretation of our findings and experiences. Conducting the research was a privilege, and we are immensely grateful to all our participants for the time they gave us and the openness with which they talked about their lives.

Outline of the book

In the chapters that follow, we discuss each of our case studies in turn. To allow for comparisons to be made between the entry route schemes, each chapter follows a consistent format and is structured in three parts. At the same time, each chapter has been written to allow for it to be read independently. Each commences with a discussion of the discursive field, and includes a national and regional policy overview, informed by our own interviews with policy makers, and a review of relevant theoretical literature. The most salient discourses dominating the particular sub-field will be identified, to enable their taken-for-granted assumptions to be deconstructed and engender a critical perspective (Morgan, 2005). This is followed by a discussion of the interventionist practices through our theoretically informed ethnographic analysis of the case study site, drawing on fieldnotes and interviews. Finally, a concluding discussion will explicate the key themes of 'getting in' and 'getting on' in context.

We start, in Chapter Two, in the North East of England with an employability training programme offered by a youth charity, many of whose clients are referred from Jobcentre Plus (the UK's government-funded employment agency and social security office found in most cities). After a brief overview of the main policy issues and labour market opportunities of the region, we use our case study organization to explore discourses of 'employability', and the tension between employability and employment in action. The chapter draws on ethnographic data of an innovative programme that is co-designed and co-delivered by young people. Our ethnography covered a period when the charity running this programme was expanding delivery and working with other organizations in the third sector to franchise the scheme. Working with these new colleagues had raised discussions about who the programme was for, and where clients needed to be on the spectrum of 'readiness' for the labour market. In our data analysis, informed by Foucault, employability emerged as an ongoing process that included both acquisition and evidence of particular skills, as well as an attitude and mental state of preparedness. Of particular concern for trainers was how to evidence the learning for their participants. Although the programme was already accredited by City and Guilds (a vocational accreditation body), the team had been working with a technology firm to offer online 'badges' for participants to work for, in order to demonstrate to employers their acquisition of cultural capital in particular areas, such as teamwork and leadership. This 'badging of the self' aptly demonstrates Foucauldian ideas of self-governance, where the self is turned into a utilitarian object that must be externally validated. Conversely, the external factors that shape labour market opportunities for these young people in this region are never part of the discussion about how to find work, revealing that, in place, 'employability' and 'employment' may be two contradictory issues.

Chapter Three moves to the South Coast of England, to explore youth enterprise training. The chapter begins with a critical overview of the policy goals of youth 'enterprise', its positioning within national and EU policy and how these are articulated at a local level on the South Coast. Once again drawing on Foucault, we interrogate the concept to demonstrate that enterprise is not just about self-employment but also about the development of the 'entrepreneurial spirit'. We use ethnographic data to explore two schemes that help to prepare young people to set up their own businesses and engage in enterprise activities. One programme is run by a third sector organization and is aimed at young people who are categorized as long-term unemployed; the other scheme is part of the offer from a higher education institution that has a prevalence of degrees that are most likely to result in freelance work or self-employed status. Through analysis of these two programmes, the chapter explores two concepts closely embedded in the notion of enterprise: risk and failure. Each programme has a very different understanding of the value of these concepts in relation to enterprise, based on its interpretation of the 'type' of young person who its programme serves. Using Foucault's notion of governmentality to consider how these young people are envisaged and constructed as entrepreneurs, the chapter argues that this is intersected by class and the young people's perceived resources and resilience.

Chapter Four shifts to London to focus on internship schemes. It commences with an overview of the contested field of unpaid internships in the UK: the policy discourses that have framed these as valuable entry route strategies for young people and the political and social controversy, and subsequent resistance, in relation to these. It then contextualizes the internship schemes involved in the research, focusing primarily on a 'blue-chip' programme offered by one of the 'Big Four' accountancy firms. This recruits (mainly middle-class) undergraduates from the UK's most elite universities for summer internships. In Foucauldian terms, these allow for early governance in the framing and positioning of work subjectivities, which, assuming the 'right sort' of performances are demonstrated, results in a firm offer of employment before graduation. In order to provide evidence of the vast diversity in the quality of internship programmes, we supplement the discussion with additional interviews conducted with young people who attended very different internships in terms of the training and work experience received. The chapter argues that the huge variance in levels of governance offered by different internship schemes delivers to the young people differing levels of exposure to risk. That those able to benefit from good governance in their training are often also well supported by family and other social networks underscores the ways that Foucauldian notions of individual and reflexive self-management vary significantly according to social class.

Chapter Five focuses on a young people's employability programme offered by a voluntary organization based in

Glasgow, Scotland. The course combines classroom-based, employability-related skills training with on-the-job work experience across a range of voluntary organizations in the city. The chapter commences with an overview of Glasgow's recent strategies to bolster youth employment opportunities for the city's young people of all educational backgrounds and how 'volunteering', based on Foucauldian notions of 'approved ways to be' in terms of employability and citizenship behaviour, has formed a key plank of policy. The chapter goes on to contextualize the training provider organization and the 'Volunteering Makes Sense' programme.[1] The ethnography, conducted within both the classroom skills sessions and the broader field of voluntary organizations where work experience is conducted, follows, drawing out the place-based nature of such placements. The chapter also argues that the liminal spaces in which the young people are located heightens the risk that they will remain on the margins of employment. In relation to this, we identify the diversity in strategies that the trainers and managers provide for the trainees to gain the behaviours as well as the cultural and social capital needed to gain secure, paid employment in a chosen field.

The final chapter draws together the case studies to pull out four key themes that have resonated throughout the analyses: regionality, social class, liminality and risk. Framed by the overarching and structuring discourse of neoliberalism, these themes dominate the opportunities and constraints facing young people chasing employment within the UK. However, while the UK is undoubtedly a distinctive context, the ways in which neoliberal market forces are framing youth employability across the Western world and beyond suggest that our findings have wider significance for youth employability policy making in other international contexts.

---

[1] We use pseudonyms for all organization names, schemes and individuals.

TWO

Employability in the North East

Introduction

This chapter explores the rise of the concept of employability and how it has influenced policy and practical interventions to address unemployment. As outlined in Chapter One, youth unemployment is a particular concern for policy makers due to the long-term scarring effects of unemployment (Bynner, 2013; EU, 2013). The liminal position of young people in society means they are often viewed as potentially dangerous if unable to access markers of adulthood, such as employment, which incorporate them into society (Mains, 2013). This chapter argues that employability is frequently utilized in neoliberalizing forms of governmentality, thereby shifting responsibility of gaining work on to the individual, rather than considering the various external and structural factors, such as availability of local work, the ability to be mobile, or affordability of childcare, that also affect employment prospects.

The chapter begins with an overview of the discourse of employability, exploring how the concept has been variously considered as a threshold of labour market readiness or, from a more processual perspective, as the need for continual skills development in a flexible labour market. It then outlines the policy context, and the various policy interventions aimed at employability generally, and for young people specifically. These have largely been focused on individual skills development, despite repeated evaluations that demonstrate they have poor outcomes and can be ineffective in enabling access to the youth labour market. Our case study of an employability programme in the North East contributes to knowledge as to why this may be so. The programme reflects the discourse of employability, but also reveals an additional complexity: the very real difficulties involved in providing support for young people who may be at very different 'distances' from entering the labour market or establishing themselves in a stable career.

Discourses of employability: labour market readiness or processual skills development?

A simple definition of 'employability' is that it is the ability to be employed. This implicitly infers that employability is an individual quest, reliant on personal skills, experiences and aptitudes (Hillage and Pollard, 1998; Peck and Theodore, 2000; Devins and Hogarth, 2005; Houston, 2005; McQuaid and Lindsay, 2005; McQuaid et al, 2005; Lindsay and Houston, 2011; Adam et al, 2017; Crisp and Powell, 2017). However, this understanding is somewhat controversial, widely criticized for neglecting the necessary and fundamental component of there being available work for someone to gain. The discourse of employability is thus far from an abstract term: it is both political and conceptual. Although much public and policy discourse represents employability as being achieved through individual upskilling and preparing young people for the labour market, we show in this chapter that employability represents and embodies a particular ideology devolved from neoliberal ideas, nested in individual responsibility and the changing role of the state in facilitating employment, that demand individuals to engage in self-governance by creating a representational 'utilitarian self' that requires external ratification.

The discourse of employability became prominent in the policy realm in the 1990s at both international and national levels in connection with active labour market policies (McQuaid and Lindsay, 2005). In the UK, employability was a key element of

New Labour's 'Third Way' policies (Peck and Theodore, 2000), and it was also evident in the European Employment Strategy, in agendas of the Organisation for Economic Co-operation and Development as part of its advocacy for active labour market policies, and at the United Nations, particularly in relation to young people (McQuaid and Lindsay 2005: 198). As McQuaid and Lindsay (2005) show, since this time, the discourse has had a number of different iterations. They demonstrate how, in narrower policy definitions, employability has come to be associated with an individual's capacity (in terms of skills, knowledge and attitude) to gain and stay in work. Employment was thus the intended outcome of economic strategies, such as Labour's New Deal (Peck and Theodore, 2000). In broader versions, McQuaid and Lindsay argue that employability can be used to overcome understandings of unemployment that focus on either, or both, supply-side and demand-side explanations (2005: 197–8). This facilitates a more 'holistic' understanding of the range of factors involved in unemployment/employment. McQuaid and Lindsay suggest that this includes not only individual factors, such as skills and mobility, as well as personal circumstances such as caring responsibilities, but also external factors, including labour market opportunities and forms of support. Despite the more comprehensive picture of unemployment/employment this approach affords, however, much policy discourse has drawn on the narrower definitions, to focus almost exclusively on individual skills and attitudes.

Partly as a function of this, employability has been deeply connected with education and training, with the latter being seen as the route to the former (Garsten and Jacobsson, 2003; Olssen and Peters, 2005). This has also been a result of the changing economy, particularly in the UK, that has shifted away from industrial manufacturing towards a knowledge economy (Brown and Lauder, 2001; Garsten and Jacobsson, 2003; Ball, 2013). Thus the forms of work for which prospective employees need to be prepared require a higher level of education.

Likewise, jobs themselves have changed, with a rise in less permanent, project-based and fixed-term contracts (Born, 2004; Grabher, 2004; Morris et al, 2010). This has meant that 'getting in' – *gaining* employment – is often not the final hurdle, and that in many sectors, the subsequent process of 'getting on' necessitates that workers must be continually looking out for the next contract.

This has also meant that there are two overlapping discourses of employability. On the one hand, employability may refer to the preparations required for 'getting in' to work, in terms of an individual's labour market readiness. Policy interventions operating with this definition intend to support individuals to acquire a set of baseline attributes (Peck and Theodore, 2000): work experience, evidence of communication and teamwork skills, basic English and mathematics qualifications, for instance. State interventions in the UK have usually not considered other factors that could determine labour market readiness such as availability of affordable childcare or the ability to move locations to available work. Alongside this, another discourse of employability emerges from the demands of a more precarious and flexible labour market (Garsten and Jacobsson, 2003; Standing, 2011). This discourse refers to a longer-term and processual form of skills development, where workers must engage in lifelong learning. This is understood to be the responsibility of workers to engage in 'career management' (Martin, 1997; Born, 2004). These two discourses coexist, and although most policy focus and intervention is on the former, the second still has demonstrable effects for workers seeking to 'get on' in their careers. Employability is thus interconnected with other neoliberal concepts, such as lifelong learning and flexibility (Garsten and Jacobsson, 2003). In the following section, we chart in more detail how employability policies have emerged in the context of the UK, and their efficacy, before turning to explore the context of our case study of employability training delivered in the North East of England.

Employability policies: the persistence of active labour market interventions

At the EU level, European countries established the European Employment Strategy in 1997, which was developed into the European 2020 Growth Strategy. It covers employment targets, research and development investment, climate change and energy, education and poverty and social exclusion – seeing these as interrelated. EU policy on youth unemployment specifically was a particular focus in the period after the 2008–12 recession, when youth unemployment rates were high across many EU countries. In 2013, all European states signed up to the EU Youth Guarantee, a commitment to provide 'a good offer of employment, continued education, apprenticeship or traineeship' (EU, 2013; European Commission, nd[a]) to under-25-year-olds within four months of unemployment or leaving education. National implementation is financially supported by the Youth Employment Initiative and European Social Fund. These funds and initiatives focus on NEETs, the long-term unemployed or those not registered as job seekers (European Commission, nd[b]). While the policy recognizes that the structural position of young people makes them more vulnerable than adults, the focus rests largely on skills development and continued education as the means of support, maintaining the discourse of individual-level interventions.

In the UK, the past four decades have seen a host of government schemes aimed at improving the employment prospects of unemployed young people. Many of these have utilized the employability discourse that individual young people need to be supported towards labour market readiness, and have focused on offering work experience, using private and third sector providers to source and manage placements. These policy interventions represent what are known as 'active labour market policies', where receipt of benefits requires participation in some form of work placement or experience. One of the first such policies began in the 1980s recession. The Community Programme offered temporary jobs for the long-term unemployed, but despite £1 billion spent, evaluations showed it had no significant effect on employment (Finn and Simmonds, 2003; Mulheirn and Rena, 2009; House of Commons Work and Pensions Committee, 2010; McGuiness and Harari, 2013). Similar schemes in later years, such as Employment Action (1991–93) resulted in similarly poor results (Finn and Simmonds, 2003; McGuiness and Harari, 2013).

The main changes to different schemes over the years and successive governments were the eligibility requirements (usually a difference in length of time claiming benefits) and length of placement. The 1993–96 scheme Community Action had somewhat better results when combining job search assistance with part-time work experience, with 14 per cent of participants finding work and 4 per cent returning to education – but these are still far from impressive. The Labour New Deals introduced in 1998 offered more choice for Job Seekers Allowance (JSA) claimants in receipt of benefits, but results differed greatly among different groups, with the poorest return for the cost of the programme among young people (National Audit Office, 2007). One report estimated that the New Deal for Young People had an effect of only 6–7 per cent (Giorgi, 2005). The 2009 Labour government's Future Jobs Fund offered all young people who had been on JSA for six months a guaranteed place in work, training or work experience, subsidized jobs that lasted at least six months for at least 25 hours a week and paid the national minimum wage. Despite successful evaluations, and indication of some long-lasting positive outcomes, it was seen as too expensive, particularly when '47% of Future Jobs Fund participants who began the Future Jobs Fund between October 2009 and March 2010 were claiming working age benefits 14 months after starting on the Future Jobs Fund' (Harari, 2011: 3).

The coalition government's 2012 Youth Contract aimed to 'support young people into sustainable employment'. The majority of the measures focused on incentivizing employers to employ under-24-year-olds, and to provide additional opportunities for JSA claimants to receive training, work experience and additional JSA adviser time. Much of the support was tailored to those who had never worked, had low qualifications or young people deemed 'NEET' (Evans, 2013), who are often considered to be the most 'problematic' group. The 2013 evaluation found that while wage incentives were not creating new jobs, they may have had an impact on employers choosing a young person over someone with similar skills. Schemes that imposed a 'mandatory work activity' as a condition of receipt of benefits had an openly acknowledged aim to work on individuals, in line with the discourse of employability that locates unemployment as the fault of the individual: 'Mandatory Work Activity is aimed at individuals deemed in need of developing good work habits and discipline, such as working under supervision and attending on time' (McGuiness and Harari, 2013: 4). While these measures had a short-term effect on the likelihood of individuals to claim benefits, there was no impact on employment, and most participants returned to claiming (Hillmore et al, 2012).

Examples of similar schemes in the 1990s in America and Australia often saw reductions in the numbers of benefit claimants, but no improvements in employment (McGuiness and Harari, 2013) Likewise, critics have argued that in a labour market of limited opportunities, training workers does not create new jobs, and positive results from job training can often be attributed to positions that would have been filled anyway, without the scheme (Lafer, 2002). In the UK's Work Programme, participants such as the retailer Poundland had to assure the public that volunteers were not replacing paid workers. But, as one of our young interviewees on the Work Programme queried, if there was work for him to do, why could it not be a real job instead of an unpaid placement? The employability discourse that underpins these schemes, with its focus on the individual, often means that interventions take little account of current labour market opportunities. As noted by several of the evaluations, labour market information and the particularities of local labour markets are very important for the success of any scheme aimed at supporting employment.

Given the lack of evidence for the efficacy of schemes of this nature, the reason they continue to persist over several decades and across different national and regional contexts must lie in the strength of the discourse of employability. This relies on an understanding of the unemployed as lacking, having a deficit in skills or work experience, and thus these schemes aim to bridge this gap by offering opportunities to gain the experience desired by employers. In our research, we aimed to explore what an employability scheme in an area of low youth labour market opportunities can offer young people and to consider what tensions arise between the discourse of employability and the realities of available employment. We next outline the context of our case study region, the North East, before describing the scheme and the organization where we conducted our research.

Employability in the North East

The North East traditionally had a local economy reliant on manufacturing. This began to decline in the 1980s, though it remains an important source of employment for the region (Hodgson and Charles, nd). Since the late 1990s, the North East has taken a proactive approach to tackling economic performance and employment as it had performed below average compared with the rest of the UK in a range of economic measures (Hodgson and Charles, nd). The success of this approach is demonstrated by the fact that the region went from being the lowest-growing region in the UK during the 1990s to one of only two regions (alongside London) to outperform national averages between 1999 and 2009 (NELEP, 2013). However, at the same time the region suffers from an absolute shortage of jobs because of too few private sector companies and jobs, and insufficient skill levels to support a modern diverse economy. Local Enterprise Partnerships (LEPs) were a coalition government policy that began in 2010, and entail private, public and education stakeholders working together to determine regional economic concerns and needs. In 2013, the North East LEP commissioned Lord Andrew Adonis to conduct an independent review of the regional economy. The report concluded that the North East needed higher-quality jobs to increase productivity and provide a broader range of training and employment opportunities for the youth workforce (Adonis, 2013). As a result, a range of initiatives have been developed by the local authorities and TSOs in the region to provide young people with the skills they need to enter the labour market.

Our key informants from the local council and the LEP explained that growth sectors in the region are the digital and creative sectors, offshore and renewables industries, manufacturing (primarily automotive) and health and life sciences. Enabling sectors include construction, professional services and education. The service sector is also consistently strong. Both key informants highlighted a mismatch between these growth areas and young peoples' aspirations:

'They're out of sync with the job market ... lots of young people have aspirations to do things, and that isn't in sync with where the opportunities might be.' (Geoff, local council)

'Our level for qualifications at the moment outstrip demand ... we are producing too many Level 4s in particular topics and we still have big vacancies in our key growth sectors ... huge amount of business administration coming out of FE [further education] colleges, we have too many hairdressers. It's that easy provision that actually we have a finite demand for at the moment ... for example we have a surplus of say fashion graduates, but we have a lack of fashion manufacturing graduates ... [In] health and life sciences, we have some great graduates coming out, what we don't have is that middle layer of technicians who could come out of FE.' (Gillian, LEP)

Geoff highlighted in particular that young people might not be aware of smaller businesses that are less able to market their opportunities. The LEP was focusing its efforts in this area, trying to work with schools, and further education and higher education institutions, to educate young people about where jobs were likely to be available and thereby influence the kinds of qualifications that they undertook:

'We have been quite vocal and quite open about where we see opportunities and the focus of labour market going, so that colleges understand what our key growth sectors are in the region and where our labour market is going so that the courses that they provide going forward actually match that demand.' (Gillian, LEP)

The LEP also played an active role in supporting schools and colleges to provide work experience by matching them up with employers.

Both NEETs and unemployment among the over-50s have been issues for the region, but improvements have been made in the employment rate of young people generally. The North East Local Enterprise Partnership (NELEP) 2014 Strategic Economic Plan (NELEP, 2014) highlighted increasing jobs, and in particular higher-level skills, and over two years, improvements were evident. However, young people were still struggling due to the mismatch between skill levels and available work. The several universities in the area could play a significant part in producing a more highly skilled workforce, although Gillian noted the need to work with universities to make sure that graduates stayed in the region rather than moving to London:

'... [It's] not a massive issue in the North East, we do have a lot of home grown graduates so they tend to go to regional universities and stay put....We've produced a suite of videos based on our smart spec sectors and the enabling sectors [using labour market information and vacancy data] to help students come out and make informed decisions about where the trends are, where the vacancies are.' (Gillian)

Gillian's desire to keep graduates in the local area is understandable, but somewhat at odds with policy interventions that seek to facilitate both job and learning mobility (European Commission, 2015). Research from other areas shows that decisions about moving outside a region involve consideration of local ties and opportunities, and are often differentiated along class lines (Jones and Jamieson, 1997; Jones, 1999; Jamieson, 2017). Mobility raises an issue with individually based definitions of employability, as availability of different jobs could mean that someone might be considered employable in one context, but not another. However, the separation between internal and external factors is not simple or clear cut. As we show later in the chapter, even local mobility between North East cities is not always possible for young people.

A further challenge of working with the post-19 cohort is tracking those who do not stay in education or who are *not* at the extreme end of need:

'... where we miss is that middle, maybe not troubled families or victims of domestic abuse or the really acute stuff that the local authorities and some of the big lottery funding tends to focus on, there's a cohort that – quite rightly – is very much supported, but there's a chunk that we miss, and I'm not convinced that we get to the bottom of that. And they're not the most acute but they still have a need, and we miss them, and I still think there is work to be done on that. But, you know, all of the funding that seems to come out of either big lottery or even some of the SFA [Skills Funding Agency] DWP [Department for Work and Pensions] funding all seems focused on that sort of most difficult cohort, and the middle sort of tranche ... that's not what the focus – certainly for European funding and things like that – has ever really been about.' (Gillian)

Recent research commissioned by London Youth highlights the significant number of 'hidden NEETs' and calls for policy strategies that approach young people holistically, recognizing the multiple factors that can influence attempts and motivation to enter work (London Youth, 2018). To a certain extent, the report recognizes that the individualizing discourse of employability can miss more complex understandings of the barriers facing young people.

The LEP was also particularly concerned about the reduction in funding that seems likely if the UK withdraws from the EU, given the levels of EU funding currently received by the region. Our case study organization deals with young people Gillian might describe as 'acute', but claims that its work is suitable for any young person, and is seeking to roll out its programme to the whole of the North East region and to different groups, such as university students and young carers. This proposed expansion of delivery raises interesting questions for the organization in relation to its understanding of employability. While it aims to be open to all young people, discussions with the new colleagues intending to franchise the programme raised questions about where young people needed to be on the spectrum of 'readiness' for the labour market in order to participate. In our data analysis, informed by our post-Foucauldian approach, employability emerged as an ongoing process that included both acquisition and evidence of particular skills, as well as an attitude and mental state of preparedness. We now turn to describe the case study organization and how its scheme sought to ready young people for the labour market by developing their employability.

Case study: Bridging the Skills Divide

Youth View North East (YVNE) is a multiple-award-winning charity that has developed a unique programme to address the issues identified by our key informants. Titled Bridging the Skills Divide (BTSD), the scheme aims to improve 'employability skills' for 16–25-year-olds. The three-week programme is distinctive, as it is co-created by employers, youth workers and young people themselves, some of whom have had personal experience of unemployment. BTSD focuses on the acquisition of soft skills and personal development and is delivered by both youth workers and young people, some having previously attended the programme themselves and have since been trained as young trainers for the programme. BTSD incorporates sessions addressing the 'employability skills' that employers cite as lacking in some young people today. These include communication, commitment, professionalism, time management, teamwork, motivation, enthusiasm and confidence. Each skill is explored through activity-based learning methods constructed to engage young people from diverse educational backgrounds and learner identities. The programme thus resonates with individual definitions of employability, but the discourse of the charity's chief executive officer and the trainers who work with the young people seeks to avoid a deficit model. One of the key tenets of the programme, as Tim, a trainer explains, is the belief that young people know the appropriate behaviours and attitudes for work. The main difficulties, as the trainers see them, are that young people lack the language to express these key ideals, and struggle to find examples of when they have demonstrated them in the past – particularly if they have not previously been in paid employment.

The teaching and learning style is deliberately different from school-based experiences, as one participant summarizes: "they try and like have a better understanding of what you want and where you want to go and not force you into something you don't want to do". The participants log their progress via self-assessment skills questionnaires and a reflective diary. On successful completion of these, through partnership with City and Guilds, each young person is awarded a Mozilla 'badge' corresponding to modules in the programme. The badges enable participants to create a digital platform showcasing their achievements for employers, providing evidence of their acquisition of skills across the key areas. In this way, the activities provide evidence and help the young people to find the language to express their understanding of employability skills and to prove their acquisition of these skills in a low-risk, low-stakes environment.

The programme thus has an outward-looking approach; even as it focused on individual skills development, it seeks to connect this to the real world and the expectations of employers, in particular in finding innovative ways for young people to gain legitimate ratifications of their skills development. Alongside this, the programme offers the chance for each young person to attend a pre- and post-training 'real life' interview with an employer. YVNE has a long-standing relationship with a local employer whose employees came to the course to conduct the interviews with the participants. The aim is that the programme culminates with a placement within a workplace setting. However, employer engagement, particularly with regard to work placements, is one of the key challenges faced by YVNE. The trainers took care to identify possible sectors based on each participant's interests. However, they often struggled to find employers willing to offer placements, either due to a perceived lack of work deemed suitable for the young people to participate in, or complications regarding health and safety (particularly in construction). Moreover, young people's interests did not always match available opportunities in the region. These difficulties are very suggestive of the structural barriers facing young people in the labour market, both in finding work experience and paid employment. If an organization that has good local networks and staff employed to find work experiences cannot source work, individuals without these resources are in a very disadvantaged position.

Ethnographic participant observation was conducted within two BTSD programmes in Hartlepool and Gateshead and a number of the young people (n = 8) were interviewed twice, during and after their programmes. The Hartlepool cohort was all male, and, reflecting the local population, white and working class. The highest qualifications among this group were General Certificates of Secondary Education (GCSEs), though some had dropped out of school before attaining qualifications. Many had been out of work and education for considerable periods, with one participant commenting during an activity that "it's been years since I picked up a pen". The Gateshead cohort was more mixed, reflecting the easy access from Newcastle, which has a more diverse population, and included migrants as well as a couple of university graduates.

Staff at YVNE confirmed that across the multiple cohorts, BTSD participants are from diverse backgrounds. While the programme is predominantly attended by local young people, 'born and bred' in the North East, participants also include migrants, both from elsewhere within the UK and from abroad, mainly from the EU. Educational backgrounds range from no or few Level 2 (GCSE) qualifications to undergraduates. Many of those with lower levels of educational qualifications have already completed other employability courses elsewhere. Others have some experience of work, usually temporary and low paid, often interspersed with spells of unpaid work and unemployment.

Some have experienced family problems, learning difficulties, mental health issues, drug and alcohol abuse and/or have criminal records. Different iterations of the scheme thus cater for both 'acute' cases as well as those who might be categorized as the 'missing middle' (Roberts, 2011), or 'hidden NEETs'.

For some, attending the programme is an attempt to make a new start, but some participants remained despondent at the commencement of the programme at the prospect of completing 'yet another employability course'. Course leaders recognize that young people come to the programme with all sorts of motivations and skill levels, but most have ambitions to find work they will enjoy as well as to attain job and economic security. Some young people require ongoing support and encouragement to attend. Motivation to continue to attend, for those sceptical at the start, comes from the activity-based learning style, the opportunity to make new friends and the expenses provided for travel and lunch for the duration of participation. Sessions have been designed with the help of young people with the deliberate aim of engaging other young people: to bring them out of their shells, enable them to recognize how much they have to offer, and help them grow in confidence and work well together.

Our interviews revealed that this approach was effective, and that the work experience was regarded as an invaluable outcome of the programme. Placements vary considerably in function and content, from working in a shop or office to having the chance to work in the creative industries through, for example, a successful partnership with a music development agency based in Newcastle. However, it was clear that the experience really can change lives, with some gaining employment as a result of their placement, and others gaining employment very soon afterwards, while those who remain unemployed often feel they are in a better position to strive for a longed-for vocation or realize there are other choices available to them.

A key component of the success of the work experience for Freddy, for example, was the new sense of respect he received. That the trainers showed real interest in his abilities and spent time attending to his skill development was highly valued, as he explains:

'I just think the respect you get, because obviously I've done courses in the past and they just treat you like shit. Like they don't put any time and effort into you, do you know what I mean? Whereas this one, like I turned up and there were so many different people that are not sort of my sort of people, if you know, and I thought "shit, I'm in the wrong place here", I felt out of place. But as time went on, like after about two weeks, like I felt like all of them were just spot on, do you know what I mean? And especially my music producer, the time and effort he put into me and the support he gave me was just unbelievable. Like I just … more than I ever thought I would get, do you know what I mean? So I really liked that.'

Freddy's narrative aligns with the external validation goals of the badging aspect of the programme, but also highlights the importance of feeling supported, an element that was also significant in the experience of young people in the volunteering programme, as we show in Chapter Five.

Although most participants enjoyed doing the various skills-based modules on the programme, some questioned just how much things would actually change in practice. As noted earlier, some know what they need to do and say at job interviews and in the workplace, but have difficulties performing in this context. The very real pressures of the workplace, compared with the relative safety of the classroom, was well recognized. A particular continuing anxiety was performing well at interview, for while Freddy was already "quite a confident person", who "wouldn't say I was 'better prepared' because I think when I do interviews and stuff I am quite good in that sort of situation", others such as Steph felt her confidence levels were "just about the same" and still felt:

'I always go in there nervous and … I know I shouldn't but I keep thinking 'what if that person in there is better than me?'

Jake agrees: "I can do it when it's not important, I can be like 'yeah I'm great I know I am' but when it comes to it I'm like 'oh, no'".

A challenge for both the trainers and the young people is the diverse starting points from which the latter come to the programme. Not only are participants at different 'distances' from the labour market, but they also have extremely different experiences of, and capability with, literacy, numeracy and public speaking. From Dave, who hasn't picked up a pen to write anything since school, to Holly, a recent graduate used to writing long essays, to Ancuta from Romania who understands very little English, trainers have no small task in involving everyone in the various classroom exercises. The activity-based learning pedagogy largely mitigates this difference, but the introduction of the badging system, which requires participants to record their learning mostly through written text, proved to be a significant challenge for some, as described later.

Critiques of active labour market strategies often rest on the accusation that they help those who are closest to labour market and who would have been likely to find work on their own anyway, without need for intervention – with some funding models accused of encouraging providers to actively target their work at this group due to the greater incentives and rewards supplied by the state (Lafer, 2002). The 'distance' of the young people to the labour market was an issue that emerged in particular in the Hartlepool programme. Given the success of the programme, YVNE has been seeking partnerships with other youth charities in the North East region that can be trained in the delivery of the scheme, thereby establishing a number of regional franchises able to reach a greater number of young people. In Hartlepool, we saw how Tim, from YVNE, who has had a leading role in BTSD, was teaching Liam and Harry to deliver the programme. This involved Tim talking Liam and Harry through the activity plans at the beginning of the day and explaining to them the learning objectives for each part. Throughout the day, Tim 'modelled' his teaching practice, allowing Liam and Harry to observe before themselves taking over and leading a session that Tim could observe and provide feedback on. The style of the sessions is interactive and aims to help young people realize how much they already know that is relevant to the workplace. Our fieldnotes demonstrate how Tim's approach helps to engage the young men in Hartlepool:

The Hartlepool group are all young men, with only one non-white participant out of 10. All are from the local area and had been unemployed for a considerable period, some since they left school. They are aged between 19 and 25. Today's sessions have focused on professional behaviours and attitudes in the work place. They have completed a number of interactive sessions together on this topic. Their first activity initially caused some consternation amongst them, as Tim, the trainer, sought to get them up off their chairs and engaging psychically as well as mentally with the content. As he explained to us later, this was to make it clear to the participants that this was not like school, at which many of their participants had often had negative experiences. Tim splits the group into two, and hands out large flipchart paper sheets, telling them to stick them together with Sellotape so that they end up with an area large enough for them to draw round one of the young people, leaving an outline. We are in a large upstairs room of a local community centre. We have been sat in a semi-circle of chairs at the front of the room, and behind these the other tables and chairs have been cleared to the back, leaving considerable free space. The two groups look at each other uncertainly, unable to even take the initiative to decide where to work, a feature of their lack of confidence which the trainers will discuss at the end of the day. Tim, noticing their indecision, takes a more direct approach – 'You go over there, you over there, lay the sheets out on the floor and stick them together with the tape.' With some help, the lads get going, and once Tim gets to the instruction for one member of the team to lay on the sheets so the others can draw around him, a couple of leaders, with more confidence to direct the others, begin to emerge. Several of them are mates from school, and a couple have never met the others before.

As they draw around their team member, to leave the outline of a body on the sheet, the lads laugh and joke with each other – particularly as when their template moves out of the way to reveal the outline, the image is rather deformed due to some baggy clothing and wobbly pen control. There are jokes about CSI (a TV show – 'crime scene investigation') and body bags. This activity seems to have worked to relax them. Tim next asks the two groups to annotate and add more drawings to the sheets – one team must draw a good employee, and the other a bad. The two teams get stuck into this activity relatively easily, bearing out YVNE's assertion that young people do know what is expected of them in the workplace. The good employee team draw a suit on their person, and add annotations such as confidence, planning, skills, team work, motivation, clear speaking, positive attitude, organised, respectful, creative thinker, honest, professional. The other team draw their bad employee with a bottle of beer, tattoos, and wearing a tracksuit and trainers (interestingly the attire of choice for all the lads during the course). Their annotations include unreliable, late, anti-social, rude, no motivation, disorganised, not cooperating and not listening to instructions. Similar activities throughout the day follow, developing this topic, including a sorting exercise where they have to match definitions with attributes such as 'organising time', 'breaking down task' and 'setting goals'.

Through activities like these, the programme directly draws on the labour market readiness discourse of employability. The young people are given the space to explore what they already know about being ready for work, to develop their confidence in their own knowledge and begin to construct ways to articulate this to employers. The newly developed badging system demonstrates that labour market readiness is no simple measure, as a conversation between Liam and Tim demonstrates. At the end of the day, the trainers sought to engage the group in completing short review tasks on what they had learnt (or realized they already knew) during the day. Liam, a youth worker, had recruited all of the participants and thus felt a strong commitment to them as individuals. Tim, while he likewise cared passionately about the young people and their outcomes, had a broader perspective about the reputation of the programme overall. Each had a different understanding of the needs of the young people and what would be of most benefit to them, which emerged during a discussion of the badging aspect of the programme, as our fieldnotes demonstrate:

At the end of the day, the young people are given the opportunity to write a short description of the key learning points from the session. Today, they have access to the community centre's computer room. Given that Dave, who left school without qualifications, and hadn't written anything since, recognisably struggled with his literacy, his summaries of the learning were often quite poor, both in terms of grammar and in comprehension. Tim reads over all the lads' shoulders, informally checking work that as part of his role, he will have to read fully and if appropriate, approve their work by awarding it a badge. Dave has frequently only written a sentence, which Tim feels is inadequate, he helps him as much as he can, but refrains from giving him the answers – this is his chance to demonstrate what he has learnt. He clearly struggles with this more formal aspect of demonstrating his knowledge, particularly with forming coherent written sentences, and gets frustrated with himself over not knowing how to spell particular words.

Liam can see his mounting frustration, and gives a bit more help, but unlike Tim, essentially gives him the right answers. Tim has to pull him aside afterwards and ask him not to do this in future. This sparks an intense discussion about the awarding of the badges, and recruitment of participants onto the programme. Liam felt that any effort from 'the lads' should be rewarded. Their experiences at school had largely not been positive, and the boost from the badges would help with their confidence and self-worth. While Tim agreed with this to a certain extent, the scheme is accredited by City&Guilds, and as such, does have a minimum standard that needs to be reached. Tim tried to explain to Liam that if everyone gets the badges, even when they do not really fully meet the conditions required, there could potentially cause problems down the line, when employers begin to view the badges. If employers see the badges as evidence of a skill, which the young person hasn't fully mastered, and this emerges post-employment, it could devalue the legitimacy and worth of the badge in the eyes of employers.

Liam argued that if the young people had been accepted onto the programme and attended the sessions, participated and completed the statements for the badges, this should be enough – what effects would it have on them to be rejected from this? Tim understood his point of view, but suggested that the issue might be about whether the young people were ready for the programme and whether they should consider a baseline to be met before participation in the programme. This was a particular concern for Tim due to the programme franchising, which meant they would have little oversight over recruitment of participants and delivery of the content. Tim and Liam come up with a temporary compromise. Tomorrow, they will get the YVNE tablets working, and they will ask the participants to fill out the summaries after each activity, rather than the end of the day, with the hope that it will help mitigate lack of recall and reinforce the learning points more immediately.

Given that the programme aims to help young people develop the ability to articulate employability skills, Tim's focus on credentialism is logical, but is also an example of the Foucauldian concept of self-governance, where the self is turned into a utilitarian object that must be externally validated. The badges represent a version of the self that is fit for outward approval, making it easier for young people to demonstrate the acquisition of desired skill sets, and for employers to identify their labour market readiness. This is often an aspect missed from discussion of employability and could be one element explaining the poor outcomes for active labour market policies such as those discussed earlier. Simply doing work experience is not enough in the contemporary, flexible labour market, whether individuals are 'getting in' to work, or 'getting on' in their careers. They must be able to articulate what they have learnt, and how they can apply those skills in a new context. A further element, and an issue evident in the experiences of the Hartlepool cohort, is the availability of work in the region, and/or the capacity of individuals to travel to work, as well as the attitudes of employers towards young people who may have complex home lives or who struggle with confidence.

Tom, who was the most able in the Hartlepool cohort and had good GCSEs, was keen to get involved in engineering and had looked into apprenticeships and further education. However, little was available in or near Hartlepool, and any opportunities he found required travelling to Newcastle. His parents' jobs prevented them from driving him, he himself did not know how to drive, and he could not afford to take driving lessons or run a car. Moreover, train travel incurred similar expense to driving and the timetables were such that he would never arrive on time. None of the employability courses and badges he could ever attain would overcome these obstacles. Likewise, Barney, in the Gateshead cohort, was incredibly shy when he began the programme, to the extent that he could not look anyone in the eye or speak even in a small group. Although his confidence improved hugely during the course of the programme, he was still very reserved and even after we had spent several days getting to know him informally, he found our interview with him very difficult. It would require a very gentle and understanding employer to take him on. Our research with YVNE showed that despite a genuine commitment to seeing things from young people's perspectives, the programme rarely tackled the external factors that shape labour market opportunities for the young people in this region, revealing that, in place, 'employability' and 'employment' may be two contradictory issues.

Discussion

Our research demonstrates how employability programmes can have clear and positive effects for individuals, as also found by Russell and colleagues (2011). BTSD's approach is, in many ways, positive and enriching for the lives of its participants. Despite this, the badges are one example of how the discourse of employability acts as a form of governmentality, shaping the self into a subjective being (Rose, 1989) through 'a specific organized practice' (McKee, 2009: 467) via external validation of an acquired skill or disposition. Through this process, young people internalize the notion that employability is an individualized process (Beck, 1992b; Beck and Beck-Gernsheim, 2002), a metaphorical 'bundle of skills' (Urciuoli, 2008: 211) they must learn to articulate. The lack of discussion within the BTSD programme about available jobs and growth sectors reinforces the individualizing discourse of employability. The evidence from this scheme also shows that, to return to McQuaid and Lindsay's point (2005), a more holistic approach is required to have a genuine impact on unemployment levels (see also London Youth, 2018).

BTSD's approach to engaging with employers has been, to a certain extent, successful. Employers were keen to tell them what skills they wanted to see in young people, and sometimes came through with work placements, and one local employer gave a not inconsiderable time investment to the pre- and post-programme interview practices. However, this does not address what McQuaid and Lindsay refer to as 'external' factors, such as the availability of work, and personal circumstances, such as an inability to drive. We would add that further external factors such as travel infrastructure and mobility also play a role in access to opportunities and support for labour market preparation. There have, therefore, been justified questions about whether employability courses are just 'place holders', which entail young people 'marking time' and 'keeping busy' rather than genuinely helping people to find work (Lafer, 2011; Russell et al, 2011; Roberman, 2014). Even with their positive impacts on confidence and self-efficacy, these schemes cannot create jobs.

Understanding discourses of employability, and how the problem of unemployment is understood and represented, is crucial to understanding how interventions are constructed and their likelihood of success. If the individualistic discourse of employability persists, issues identified by our key informants, such as the importance of using labour market information to educate young people about what work is available, and to tailor educational and training offers with this in mind, are eclipsed by a supply-side focus only. Alongside this, it is crucial to consider the way in which these schemes are monitored and evaluated. The discussion between Tim and Liam reveals the potential for organizational goals to conflict with the needs of individual participants. If, like other labour market activation schemes (see Lafer, 2011), BTSD becomes judged (with continued funding potentially being reliant on these judgements) by the number of young people achieving badges, the ability of YVNE to cater for all young people, no matter their distance from the labour market, becomes untenable. Those 'acute' and 'not acute enough' cohorts that our key informant Gillian mentions might be left behind. It is through accountability measures such as this that employability schemes become co-opted by and replicate neoliberal discourses (Wilde, 2016).

THREE

Enterprise on the South Coast

Introduction

This chapter explores the discourses of enterprise, uncovering the investment in this notion at EU, national and local levels of policy as a solution to youth unemployment. We present two different interventions on the South Coast that aim to increase youth enterprise. These schemes articulate resonating, but significantly different, discourses of enterprise and entrepreneurs. Risk and failure are closely embedded in both discourses of enterprise, but the two interventions have a very different understanding of the value of these in relation to their interpretation of the 'type' of young person they cater for. At South East University (SEU), a university-organized bootcamp aimed at students and graduates likely to work in fields that commonly employ freelancers, we found that failure is seen as a normal and important part of learning, and something that participants should embrace. In contrast, at Enterprising Youth, a third sector scheme aimed at the long-term unemployed, failure is viewed almost wholly negatively, and the training puts emphasis on ensuring that participants understand the risks and 'realities' of enterprise.

Using Foucault's notion of governmentality to consider how these young people are envisaged and constructed as entrepreneurs through notions of risk and failure, we argue that these different understandings of the young people rest on the fact that the focus of the training utilizes different technologies of governance. Foucault defined four different technologies:

(1) technologies of production, which permit us to produce, transform, or manipulate things; (2) technologies of sign systems, which permit us to use signs, meanings, symbols, or signification; (3) technologies of power, which determine the conduct of individuals and submit them to certain ends or domination, an objectivizing of the subject; (4) technologies of the self, which permit individuals to effect by their own means or with the help of others a certain number of operations on their own bodies and souls, thoughts, conduct, and way of being. (Foucault, 1988: 18, cited in Deetz, 1998: 152)

While these interconnect and overlap, the differentiation is helpful for understanding and explaining the difference in the approaches that existed between the two enterprise programmes we investigated, and the subtly distinct notions of enterprise that arose. SEU aims to encourage a form of enterprise that occupies the dominant discourse within the public imagination – that of ground-breaking innovator with the young person at the centre. Thus, its training focuses on developing the self, utilizes technologies of the self, and represents the most neoliberal intervention we encountered across the four schemes detailed in this book. At Enterprising Youth, the young people are perceived to be developing more traditional businesses, and the training has a more supportive approach focused on helping participants understand the key features of running a small business, the training thus operating primarily through technologies of production. SEU's approach represents a greater penetration of neoliberal ideas, as it embodies the notion of the individual as the locus of responsibility and change. Before describing the learning activities on these programmes and how they represent different technologies of governance, we first explore more fully the broader discourses of enterprise, and then trace these through EU, national and local policies to set the context in which these the two providers operate.

Discourses of enterprise: a driver of economic growth and an innovative 'mindset'

Enterprise is a multifaceted term, used partly as a synonym for business in general, but often used to signify the establishment of a new business. Alongside this, enterprise is also used to represent a particular 'mindset' and to indicate a set of moral values (Caird, 1990). As a concept, enterprise is intimately connected to neoliberalism, as it similarly relies on two of the fundamental 'promises' of neoliberalism: individual freedom and choice (Harvey, 2005). Enterprise offers individuals the freedom to shape their own working lives and to have choice over their working hours and colleagues. For policy makers, it reduces the need for state support for employment, as it requires individuals to develop and find their own income sources. Businesses that grow can offer further employment opportunities for others. Enterprise therefore embodies neoliberal policies and practices that seek greater individualization and responsibilization for work and employment. As neoliberal discourses have increasingly shifted responsibility from the state to the individual, a concurrent transfer of risk on to individuals has occurred. This is particularly evident for individuals engaged in enterprise activities. As well as the financial risks involved in not having a guaranteed salary, self-employed people are not entitled to a range of employment benefits such as parental leave, sick and holiday pay, and it is often challenging for them to invest in a pension scheme.

At EU, national and local policy levels, discourses of enterprise operate on two planes. The first is in relation to economic goals. In 2004, Action Plan: The European Agenda for Entrepreneurship claimed that:

> Entrepreneurship is a major driver of innovation, competitiveness and growth ... A positive and robust correlation between entrepreneurship and economic performance has been found in terms of growth, firm

survival, innovation, employment creation, technological change, productivity increases and exports ... (European Commission, 2004: 3)

By 2013, the EU action plan still emphasizes economic goals, but due to the (then) recent economic crisis and ensuing high unemployment levels, the emphasis is more focused on enterprise as a means of job creation.

Underlying these pragmatic aims, the second plane of the enterprise discourse is in terms of individual workers' personality traits. Entrepreneurship is seen to require a particular 'mindset', usually associated with risk taking and innovation. Thus, the European Commission argues that to increase enterprise activities a '... more entrepreneurial mindset is needed. This means actively promoting *entrepreneurial values* and addressing the fear of *risk-taking* among the widest possible audience of potential entrepreneurs' (European Commission, 2004: 4, emphasis in original). In 2013, the definition of an entrepreneurial mindset is expanded to include: 'creativity, initiative, tenacity, teamwork, understanding of risk and a sense of responsibility. This is the entrepreneurial mind-set that helps entrepreneurs transform ideas into action' (European Commission, 2013: 6). The 2013 action plan also has a greater emphasis on entrepreneurship education and, in particular, the role of higher education institutions in its provision.

Previous research has also bifurcated along these two lines: on the one hand pursuing macro-level perspectives that consider the impact and contribution of enterprise to economies (Waring and Brierton, 2011; White, 2017), and on the other hand investigating which individual traits and aptitudes engender successful enterprises (Johnson, 1988; Athayde, 2009; Smith et al, 2014) and the effectiveness of enterprise education in teaching these (Johnson, 1988; Caird, 1990; Shutt and Sutherland, 2003; Johansen, 2013; Young, 2014). The aim here is often to understand which factors influence enterprise start-ups, and what kinds of influences or education programmes increase these and improve survival rates. For example, Curran and Blackburn (1990) found that factors influencing young people's motivations to start businesses were gender, location (that is, potential market), parental experiences of enterprise and social class. Meager and colleagues' (2003) evaluative study of a youth enterprise scheme discovered that older, more educated youth participants, who had familial experiences of enterprise, were more likely to have surviving businesses. Other research has explored the motivations for enterprise more qualitatively, with indications that enterprise represents an escape from precarious labour markets (Wilkinson, 1997, cited in Du Bois-Reymond, 1998), or enables more flexible working lives, which is often a significant motivator for young parents and particularly women (Green and Cohen, 1995; Marler and Moen, 2005; Bunk et al, 2012; Hilbrecht and Lero, 2014; Bögenhold and Klinglmair, 2015). Interestingly, Meager and colleagues (2003) found that those who were motivated by independence and lifestyle choices, rather than growth or income, were more likely to continue trading.

In previous work, we have argued that gender and life stage play a key role in the motivations and ambitions of young entrepreneurs, as well as their levels of material success (Wilde and Leonard, 2018). While the young men in our sample saw themselves as archetypal entrepreneurs, had bold ideas and were willing to take risks, the young women were more measured, some might argue more realistic, in the scope of their ambitions. We found that despite the importance of gender and life stage to ambition, the young people's structurally disadvantaged positions were the most significant feature of why the move into self-employment did not tend to increase their economic stability as they hoped. Thus, in contrast to policy discourses, 'mindset' may not be the main determining factor for the increase and survival of enterprise activities, although there is likely a correlation between believing enterprise is a possibility, and structural factors such as gender, age and class.

In spite of this socio-structural reality however, the notion that successful entrepreneurs are those individuals who take risks inflects policy discourses on youth enterprise. Enterprise is seen to require a space 'where you are allowed to fail and take risks' (NYA, 2015: 10). For young people with children, or those with no familial safety net, there is potentially a lower capacity for risk and a more visceral aversion to failure. Contrastingly, for those participants with family resources to support them, the consequences of failure may be less acute. The significance of such insights for policy means that interventions that seek to target 'mindset' may not be as effective as recognizing the structural elements that influence individuals and targeting intervention activities at that level instead of the individual, in a similar way that individualized employability measures neglect structural barriers, as argued in Chapter Two.

The policy context of enterprise: a solution to youth unemployment?

The notion of enterprise strikes at the heart of broader policy discussions about the levels of responsibility of individuals, and the role of the state in the former. At the EU level, suggested policy interventions are organized into two main areas that map against the two planes of enterprise discourse discussed earlier. For economic growth, the EU makes recommendations about how to create an encouraging economic environment through access to finance and decreased regulation, particularly for small and medium-sized enterprises. In terms of developing entrepreneurial mindset, the EU makes proposals about training, and the use of role models to encourage under-represented groups such as women and ethnic minorities (European Commission 2004, 2013).

In the UK, enterprise has long been a key theme of government for both young people and adults (Keat and

Abercrombie, 1991; Cohen and Musson, 2000), particularly with regard to the 'mindset' plane. In the 1980s, government policy sought to address the 'so-called "dependency culture"' (MacDonald, 1991: 255), where individuals were considered to be over-reliant on the state and, instead, needed to build 'Victorian values of self-reliance and individual responsibility' (MacDonald, 1991: 256). This was carried through into New Labour's New Deal welfare-to-work policies, which shifted state benefits from being unconditional to requiring individuals to engage in forms of work as a condition of aid, as explored in Chapter Two (Finn, 2000; Sunley et al, 2001). The 2001 New Deal aimed to increase individual enterprise activities, with the argument that this would be more effective towards improving unemployment levels than benefits alone (Shutt and Sutherland, 2003).

With the 2008–12 economic recession disproportionately affecting the youth labour market and young people struggling to find work that offered a liveable wage, stability and progression opportunities, a range of employability interventions, such as the Youth Contract, were developed to help them into work (House of Commons, 2012). Enterprise emerged as a particularly appealing policy 'solution' to the unemployment of young people from all educational backgrounds (Brewis et al, 2010), and efforts to develop entrepreneurial traits and activities in young people have been a key policy focus (Young, 2014; NYA, 2015). The 2010–15 coalition government thus introduced an array of state-funded initiatives to increase enterprise among young people, such as providing start-up loans for 18–30-year-olds, recruiting Enterprise Champions to visit schools and supporting a Global Entrepreneurship Week, co-run by a youth charity.

The political discourse reflects the aim of inducing a mindset, as David Cameron describes in his speech to the Conservative Conference in 2011:

I want to focus on another value that runs deep, really deep in this party. It's about the hunger to get on in life. The spark of initiative. The courage to make your dream happen. The hard work to see it through. I'm talking about enterprise. Enterprise is vital for our economy – we all know that. (Cameron, 2011)

After the Conservative Party took over from the coalition government in 2015, the commitment to business creation was maintained. Sajid Javid MP, the Minister for Business, Innovation and Skills, expressed the link between enterprise and the economy as:

Economic growth comes from one thing and one thing alone. Successful private businesses. The role of government is to create an environment in which private business can thrive ... when they create businesses they create jobs. They create prosperity. They create opportunity. Businessmen and women are the heroes of Britain's economic recovery. (Javid, 2016)

These sentiments are also evident in the government's Industrial Strategy (BEIS, 2017) and 2018 Budget (UK Government, nd) through measures such as those recommended by the EU action plans, to reduce regulation and increase financing opportunities. In the 2013 European Commission report (2013), after an EU-wide decrease in business start-up rates, there is a greater emphasis on entrepreneurship education as a way to encourage an understanding of risks and thereby boost employment. This was echoed by the then Prime Minister Theresa May in 2017:

... we will always back enterprising small and medium-sized business owners. They are people who take risks with their own economic security in order to start and grow a business, contribute to our national success and provide employment to other people. They don't play it safe – they put faith in their talent and hard work and take a chance. When they succeed, we all benefit. So as aspiration becomes reality, as an idea becomes an invoice, we will back those who dare to dream and who dare to think big. (May, 2017)

Evidence of the efficacy of enterprise schemes is regarded as small scale, and lacking in rigour (Halabisky et al, 2012; Green, 2013). As we argued previously, the measures used to consider 'success' of enterprise initiatives often focus on data such as numbers of new businesses, which tell us little about the material circumstances of entrepreneurs (Wilde and Leonard, 2018). In the academic literature, there is considerable evidence to suggest that 'the entrepreneur' often emerges as a romantic figure who is adventurous, shrewd and pragmatic and takes risks (Bruni et al, 2004; Ahl, 2006;). However, the characterization of risk taking as a fundamental part of enterprise may not even be accurate: Greene and Storey's (2005) longitudinal survey evaluating a youth enterprise scheme found that those who were averse or neutral to risk were actually more likely to stay in business. At the EU and national levels, enterprise has been billed as a policy solution to economic problems and unemployment figures and, for this, a specific attitude is seen to be essential: to be 'entrepreneurial', to 'think big', and to create innovative solutions, new products and new market opportunities. We now turn to explore how this discourse emerges in programmes aimed at young people on the South Coast.

Enterprise on the South Coast

The rationale for conducting research in the city of 'Coastal' on the South Coast was its comparably high level of youth employment in 2014 (Crowley and Cominetti, 2014). We were interested to see if this was the result of local policies or economic opportunities that might differ from the other regions in our sample. We conducted five interviews with key informants to gain an understanding of local labour market opportunities for young people. Karen, one of our key informants who worked at SEU, explained that the region has four main work sectors: marine and maritime; science, technology, engineering and mathematics (STEM); retail; and the public sector. Each presents unique challenges to the city and neighbouring regions. Several of these sectors comprise a few firms employing a large number of workers who would be vulnerable if their employers went into decline. STEM, it was noted, has an ageing workforce with many employees looking to move into managerial positions, requiring upskilling, but with a lack of low-skilled entrants to the sector to fill the gap of their upward trajectory. In contrast, the retail sector is expanding and has an ample supply of low-skilled workers from the several universities in the area, but requires managers who are often brought in from outside because of lack of skills in the region. Government public sector cuts have also made this sector less reliable as an employer for the local economy:

'... there's too many students anyway so they're always going to be able to recruit low value job staff. The biggest issue is that the majority of retail chains will bring their middle management from elsewhere, and so what you've actually got is an opportunity there for the junior management levels, but they're not recruiting locally, they're bringing them in from outside ... there's a skills issue there, because they actually wouldn't bring them in from outside if they could avoid it, but we don't have people at managerial level in retail in the city.' (Karen)

Coastal is thus dealing with similar issues of gaps in skills as the North East, discussed in Chapter Two. As another key informant from the LEP explained:

> 'We have created a lot of jobs coming out of the recession and we've got fairly low unemployment rates, but our productivity is below the national average, by 5 per cent … what we've got is a lot of low wage, low skilled jobs … [for the higher skilled jobs] you find that you get an influx of sort of leafy [region], you know they don't live here, they commute in.'

The region has available low-skilled work, but lacks opportunities for stable, well-paid work with potential for progression. This is particularly the case for local young people with no/low-level qualifications who are competing with better qualified students and graduates who come to study at the universities in the region (Green et al, 2015).

Coastal's LEP wrote the local economic growth plan and is responsible for managing funds from a government city deal, a local growth deal and the EU. Enterprise is a strategic priority of its work as it is seen as being able to create a less-exposed labour market by diversifying labour market opportunities. Thus, the LEP promotes a number of initiatives to encourage and support new businesses start-ups. According to the LEP (NELEP Review Team 2013), the recession had a particularly detrimental impact on the region's businesses, with numbers of new start-ups and their survival rates dropping by several points between 2007 and 2011. The LEP's plan offers support and hopes that by 'expanding enterprise culture' it can diversify the employment offering for everyone in the region. To achieve this, the LEP explicitly states working with the third sector, such as Enterprising Youth, as a key objective. Mapping to both EU and national policy interventions, the LEP has also offered its own start-up loan scheme to try to tackle the lack of local access to skilled work. There is a strong focus on enterprise education, and the need for this to be embedded into curriculums where graduates are likely to be self-employed or freelance. Through these measures, the LEP hopes to support the creation of 1,000 new businesses and improve their survival rate. The two interventions that we chose to focus on in the region may cater for two quite different groups of young people, but, as we now show, both are seeking to operationalize these policy discourses as interventions and encourage more start-ups among young people.

Case study: SEU Enterprise Bootcamp

SEU is a teaching-focused, post-92 university, with an active widening participation policy. Many programmes are more geared towards particular career fields than traditional university subjects commonly found at Russell Group institutions.[1] SEU has a specialist Enterprise Unit in recognition of the fact that many students will enter freelance roles. Students are also more likely to be state-educated and first-generation entrants. One of our key informants, Karen, the head of the Enterprise Unit explained:

'95 per cent of our students are from state schools; 63 per cent are first entrants, so their parents were not at university.... 32 per cent are from non-traditional or disadvantaged postcodes ... we tend to have more creative

---

[1]   Post-1992 universities are institutions that were given university status as part of the Further and Higher Education Act 1992, or since this time. The Russell Group is a consortium of research-intensive universities that formed to represent their interests. These institutions tend to have higher entry tariffs than post-1992 universities and gain a greater proportion of research funding.

graduates here than anywhere else … we are a new university… we are a Widening Participation institution … we have very little research and we're not in the top 20 for anything – apart from the measures of student enterprise and student start-up companies.'

As well as specific schemes for students and graduates, such as training, mentoring and financial support, SEU also embeds enterprise into the curriculum, partly in response to student demand and the nature of the degrees offered. The unit has a range of functions at the university, supporting teaching colleagues to embed enterprise in their curriculums, as well as managing a hub for students and graduates to access a range of resources such as market research databases. Karen and her colleague John suggested that we could best gain an understanding of the work they did with students by attending an Enterprise Bootcamp weekend, an initiative aimed at supporting students to turn their ideas into reality by giving them the confidence to go out and start trading their product or service. Students sign up in advance and attend for two days; after this they are invited to join the Enterprise Society and to access mentoring. The bootcamps have an explicit focus on innovation and tap directly into the romantic ideal of 'the entrepreneur' as a go-getting risk taker.

John delivers many of the programmes at SEU and comments that one of the rationales for the Enterprise Unit is increasing awareness of entrepreneurship and demand from young people to start their own businesses. He also felt that the unit stems from the type of degree that are on offer to students:

'I think there's something about the courses we do here which are – I won't use that word vocational – but they are sort of practical, hands-on, that would lead themselves to definitely getting a freelancing kind of career. So,

I think we're pushing a relatively open door in terms of our student profile.'

There was also a keenly felt responsibility to the local area, which drew directly on local policy discourses regarding increasing the number of business start-ups in the region:

'We do the best we can to help the city ... 40 per cent of the students stay in the city, so 60 per cent move on to London. And obviously the more we can encourage ... through giving them formal support, that means they might start an office here, they might kick off their businesses here. The council and the Chamber of Commerce just love to hear that, so we do try very hard with incubation units and practical office support and that kind of thing. Coastal as a city needs that support because, you know traditionally we have quite a strong employment rate compared ... we've been relatively lucky ... but the more we can do for the city the better, because the start-up rate is relatively low across the city, we're quite low down in terms of total economic activity.'

The programmes designed by SEU are based on a four-step model: Ideation – Formation – Practice – Competency. Although students were seen to have individual journeys and might approach the unit at different points along the journey, characteristically 'acting on ideas' was often the trickiest part, and as such this provided the motivation for the bootcamps:

'...when you've got students, quite a lot of them will get stuck on Formation. So, they'll have an idea and they'll practice it a little bit in the context of their course, and then they won't actually put that into, either into practice or get their heads around what the practice means. Because quite often they'll play at it but they won't commit to it. And it's that mental commitment that they have an issue with.' (Karen)

A key concern for the unit was therefore to urge students to try out enterprise while they had the security of a student loan to support them:

'How do we get more of the students who are doing the freelancing to actually get themselves understanding that they can do it. Because one of the things we know is if they start up their business in the second year then they have a reasonable chance of being stable by the time they finish their third year, even if they've only done a little bit of work, if they can actually manage to turn a profit on any of the work that they've done between the middle of the second year and the end of the third year – and that shouldn't have to impact any of their work, all they need is three or four customers, because it's that practice and that takes them down the line of competency – then we've got a reasonable chance that they will then at that point recognise that they can freelance. And the other thing as well that they don't understand is that immediately you've finished being a student you've got no longer free money, and so actually … using the student loan as a boot-strapping, is fantastically valuable.' (Karen)

This lowers the risk, as students are not reliant on their enterprise activities to get by, offering them a zone to test the required practices and move towards competency. Alongside providing a testing space (often with small pots of funding), the unit aims to prepare students for the realities of self-employed, freelance work:

'... you need to embed a dose of realism, experiential realism "this is what it's going to be like" without having them running down the road crying "oh I couldn't possibly do that".... So it's a little balance between knowing, you know, "if you don't sell anything you won't have any income", and just getting that realism and getting them to think "OK I've got to be professional to do this, but what have I got to do to be professional".' (John)

This often requires what Karen calls 'pre-pre-start':

'... you have pre-thought and then action and then reflection and then relapse.... Well it's pretty much the same in small businesses, but with students you end up with pre-pre-start, because in reality they aren't at the stage that most people are. So if they've come straight through the school system and they've done nothing else, they've got no experience of life and so they don't know what will work and what won't work, whereas the rest of us just learn it a little bit you know.' (Karen)

'Yes, their business idea will be restricted to the square mile around the student as well.... And there's where it comes back to the entrepreneur journey, because as Karen was saying if you know what stage they are, those four new stages that we had, then you can take them to learning, I think, but not for what demographic they are but what stage of the journey.' (John)

These perceptions that young people are keen to start businesses, are pursuing degrees that are likely to result in freelance or self-employed forms of work, and are at different points on a journey, clearly influenced the provision from the Enterprise Unit. In November 2014, we observed an Enterprise Bootcamp weekend. Over two days many of the workshop activities and discussions focused on helping the young people to understand their own selves, their own ways of working and what kinds of traits and attributes would make them successful, as our fieldnotes demonstrate:

On our first morning at the Enterprise Bootcamp at SEU, we arrive to find 14 students sitting around a large rectangular table. Only two are female. We receive a short speech from John about the aims of the weekend – to 'meet like-minded people, get the confidence to finalise your idea, and inspire you to give it a go' and the students are then each given a thirty-second pitch to introduce who they are, their business idea and what they are here for. Students at all stages of their degrees, as well as graduates are represented, studying subjects including IT, business management and sport. Interestingly, less than half have a clear business idea already. John introduces the next activity:

'The most successful entrepreneurs understand themselves, we can't do everything, so what are you good at? This session will help you think about your strengths and weaknesses, so that you can understand yourself and how others are similar or different. There is no right or wrong, this is to help you understand how you work with others and overcome difficulties.'

John hands out a questionnaire, telling the participants to fill it out quickly, without thinking too much about the answers. The form is divided into short lists of four attributes, from which the participants must pick the closest descriptor applying to themselves, or two if they can't decide.

Figure 1: Reproduction of personality attributes, SEU bootcamp activity

__logical __persuasive __sociable __loyal	__cheerful __business-like __detailed __good listener	__messy __deep __tactless __plain	__hard to please __argumentative __disorganized __follower
__optimistic __willing __fussy __stubborn	__serious __peaceful __popular __competitive	__dependable __funny __positive __respectful	__friendly __lively __confident __organized
__talkative __pessimistic __shy __bold	__timid __restless __domineering __moody	__forceful __hesitant __unpredictable __withdrawn	__productive __accurate __convincing __compromising
__risk taker __lenient __loner __worrier	__planner __supportive __leader __excitable	__submissive __haphazard __outspoken __persistent	__scheduled __gentle __daring __loud
__perfectionist __proud __forgetful __reserved	__impatient __orderly __changeable __doubtful	__mixes easily __task-orientated __agreeable __systematic	__strong-willed __inconsistent __reluctant __critical
__patient __decisive __enthusiastic __well behaved	__interrupts __short-tempered __stuffy __serene	__considerate __promoter __independent __introvert	__undisciplined __idealistic __thorough __good-natured

After filling out the questionnaire, each participant adds up their score and is given a total which places them into a 'social style' – Expressive, Amiable, Driver or Analyst. John then encourages each group to discuss their three strengths, three weaknesses, decide on a motto and two of their social style's characteristics that they find difficult.

After identifying their own social style, and its strengths and weaknesses John then applies this to a research paper outlining what makes entrepreneurs entrepreneurial. He goes through each of the points made by the author, giving tips about how if they are a particular type, they should respond to Sarasvathy's advice (2008). A key aspect of his talk emphasises the necessity of trying things out, learning from mistakes, and being willing to fail and have another go. Thus expressions such as 'fail forward', 'affordable loss principle', 'deal with failure and start again', 'expect and embrace uncertainty', 'get to market quick, to learn' 'have the courage to fail' feature prominently in the discourse of the programme.

The activities at the bootcamp focus a great deal on the notion of 'turning ideas into action' through understanding and working on the self. In one activity on the second day, with the theme of 'taking your product to market', the focus is on how the participants' strengths will enable them to do this. As evidenced in the narratives of John and Karen, the aim is to help students believe that they can be entrepreneurs. The main technologies of governance in the learning activities are those of the self – 'operations on their own bodies and souls, thoughts, conduct, and way of being' (Foucault, 1988: 18, cited in Deetz, 1998: 152). The activities aim to engender belief through action, as quickly as possible, ideally while the students still have the safety net of their student loans to bankroll their activities.

Case study: Enterprising Youth programme

In contrast to the SEU bootcamp, Enterprising Youth (EY) is run by a charity and has been active for many years. The course is aimed specifically at young people who have been unemployed for at least six months, defined as working under 16 hours a week. An initial four-day course introduces participants to the 'pros and cons' of self-employment and running a business. After the course, participants are allocated an experienced mentor to guide them through developing a business plan or support them into another route if they decide against self-employment. They have up to 12 months to prepare their plan, which they can submit to a business panel for small-grant funding in order to test their product or service and/or access continued mentoring support. Loans of up to £2,000 are also available, and although credit checks are conducted, EY will consider applicants with poor credit ratings, if they prove that they can pay back their debts during the three months prior to application. Despite being billed as 'enterprise', the course focuses on more traditional and gendered forms of self-employment, with a garage and hairdressers the two example businesses used in exercises, rather than more romantic or innovative approaches usually associated with the term 'enterprise' (Curran and Blackburn, 1990).

The discourse takes a different tone at EY from the one at SEU, and the technologies of governance focus far more on the practical and logistical elements of running a business in the long term, rather than a desire to turn idea into action as soon as possible. The regional manager, Gary, tells us the participants attracted to EY have often not been successful in education and have struggled to find work:

> 'Probably a third, if not more, were educational underachievers, they had less than five GCSES A-C ... over a third ... have a learning difficulty ... And they plumped for self-employment for two reasons, firstly they're not particularly attractive to mainstream employers in what is a very competitive market, and secondly, they had the Jobcentre pushing them to get off benefit.'

Thus, in Gary's view, rather than enterprise being an active choice and an exciting and positive option for young people, as was the view at SEU, for those on EY courses, self-employment was a fall-back option when they had been unsuccessful in other realms. Likewise, Judy, one of the volunteer mentors and a retired marketing executive, explains that the young people have to be determined, and only about 20 per cent of the participants both choose to carry on and are then successful in their business ventures:

'They are young people who are already self-motivated and who have decided they want to work for themselves and have a business idea that they believe they can make [work] ... The purpose of the course is first of all the make sure that they've actually thought through why they really want to work for themselves, and ... the figures are something like one in four really makes a go of it ... that's successful and which supports them and where very often they can offer employment to other people.'

Of those who continue, the levels of success are variable. Judy says:

'About one in four really does well and creates a viable and sustainable business strong enough to employ other people. About two out of four bumps along, you know, off benefits by and large, and working, you know, feeling fairly good about themselves. And one in four bombs completely ... goes back on benefits or gets into some sort of trouble ... I think it's a great programme. I don't think it will ever get 100 per cent success rate because people are people and they're hugely variable in their behaviour.'

At SEU, there is a considerable focus on the importance of failure as way of learning, and Karen and John encourage their participants to try things out as soon as they can. In comparison, Gary and Judy at EY are more cautious and risk averse. They are more circumspect about the likelihood of their participants' success and Gary spoke a few times about how, over the years, they had learnt more about not 'setting people up to fail' by offering funds for ventures when participants were not ready or capable of succeeding.

The EY trainers spent more time than the SEU bootcamp trainers discussing the young people's business ideas and their viability. For example, on the second day of the EY course Judy focused on marketing and selling. Although Gary had previously informed us that most participants had low levels of education, five of the participants in the session we attended had been to university, although three had never completed their degrees. The following extract is from our fieldnotes:

Judy starts the day by asking each of the participants to give an explanation of their business ideas. We learn that Lily aims to start a ballet costume design and manufacturing business, James and Sam are business partners wanting to design video games, Palmer intends to start the new 'Student ebay', where they can trade textbooks, Bryony has a new method of applying hair extensions, Grace wants to produce a line of creativity enhancing children's toys and Stewart intends to deal in second hand goods. As they explain their ideas, Judy asks probing questions about their background experience in these fields. She listens carefully and gives nothing away about what she thinks of their ideas at this stage, there is no hint of encouragement, unlike John's very effusive style of praise at SEU. Judy continues the introduction to marketing by explaining most marketing textbooks are structured around the 'four Ps'. She asks if anyone has heard of these. Two participants, Sam and Palmer, who both attended business courses at university say that they have. Judy writes these up on the flipchart paper mounted on the wall; Product, Price, Place, Promotion. Underneath this she writes, BRAND.

Judy leads a group discussion on what a brand is, asking the participants to suggest brands that come to mind and discussing what characterises the 'personality' or 'identity' of each one that they call out. Judy concludes this part of the session by summarising that a brand is the identity that you want to create for your business, and is usually based on a set of values and linked to those who you want to reach, for whom those values are also important. She then puts them into pairs and asks them to think of three values that they would want identified with their brand, and how they could achieve this. Sessions later in the day cover how to price their products in relation to other brands so that they are targeting the right market, and developing an understanding of your typical customer through market research.

Thus the key points of day two are about encouraging participants to think very specifically about their business development and understanding the market that they want to enter: a technology of governance that focuses on production, the ability to 'produce, transform, or manipulate things' (Foucault, 1988: 18, cited in Deetz, 1998:152).

At EY, the young people's business ideas are under primary scrutiny. In the trainers' view here, preparing the business plan is the most important thing for the young people to be getting on with – it is, after all, how they will finance their ideas, so it remains the focus of the course. This is seen as a long–term plan, with a need for strategy and careful thought. The aim is to avoid risk, rather than to move into action. This stems from the experience the trainers have had in supporting young people in the past, and their desire to make sure that participants do not experience additional failures, given that for many of them, self-employment is an escape from a precarious labour market in which they have already been unsuccessful.

This focus on the business idea was valued by the participants, even if they also found it frustrating having to wait, think more and conduct research before executing their ideas. Lily, who trained as a ballet dancer but struggled to make enough money as a professional dancer, wanted to produce unique dance wear, and the structure of producing a business plan and undertaking market research helped her consider whether the business would provide her with enough income:

'I really want to get going so I'm always wanting to do things like straightaway … It actually gave me a good idea, because before I went I was a bit confused … really thinking about all the things that I need to think about and how to move forward in the future … I think it opened my eyes, you know especially as business is about making a profit as well, and thinking of ways to make it profitable.'

Stewart, who wanted to open a second-hand goods shop, had a similar experience after spending time looking into the costs of renting retail space:

'The way I was going to go … everything's changed slightly. But my first priority call was just to set up shop straightaway, sell everything as much as possible, and then just see how the business would go. I'm now looking to setting up online first.'

While Stewart's approach would have been valued at SEU, at EY he was cautioned against taking on too much at once. Sam also found the mentor's probing helpful for considering risk in decision making:

'[My business partner and I] have the trap of kind of going in a direction which is wrong, but we're so confident in what we're doing we just go ahead with it. But now that we've got a mentor, they're questioning us on everything we do … we could be too arrogant and we just go full steam ahead into a situation without realising some of the threats and risks, and then we've got this guy going "sorry, why are you actually doing this?".'

Gary explained that "one of the things that's very hard for us on Enterprising Youth is to what extent to be encouraging, and to what extent to be realistic". He further explained that many of the young people had big ideas and dreams, but these motivations were not always grounded in the realities of self-employment, particularly in terms of the profits that could be expected in the first few years. For Gary, it was important that the young people understood they had to "support themselves while they're trying to create their dream". In another exercise recorded in our fieldnotes, he asks them to complete a 'survival budget':

> He explains to the group that businesses that just break even are often not factoring in most of their own labour costs, and people end up working for £2.50 an hour, as an example. He challenged the group to think about what would count as being 'successful', asking participants to consider whether that is enough for them, would it be better to get a job somewhere else, or could they put up with earning so little, even if they loved doing it? 'I know it might bore the socks off you, but would you do a cashier job for £2.50 an hour?'

> To bring the realities home to participants, they must complete a 'survival budget' by calculating the basic funds that they would need to survive per week. Gary is keen to make sure this is about the absolute necessities. This does not take into account quality of life per se, though some suggestions were made about things that might be given up, such as smoking or a Friday night drink with friends.

The young people's ability with money is also a cause for concern, as the survival budget example makes clear – they have to be able to manage their behaviour in order to qualify for funding and not carry any debts. There is an implicit understanding on the part of the trainers about how these young people should be conducting themselves, and the kinds of things that they should be spending their money on. Thus, in addition to the technologies of production, technologies of the self are also evident over the course of the programme. But this does not form the core of the learning objectives. The viability of the business idea, the plan and participants' ability to put it into action (such as their abilities to market and sell their product or service) are also considered to be vital. In contrast, at the SEU bootcamp weekend, the business ideas are less discussed; instead, emphasis is placed on participants' selves and on understanding who they are and how they work best.

In both contexts, risk and failure feature prominently, but the two providers have very different perceptions of their participants' ability to cope with and weather uncertainty. The EY participants are vulnerable, they do not have family resources to fall back on, and they have already been unemployed for at least half a year. The SEU students have their student loans to support them and are encouraged to consider the resources available to them in terms of the networks they are developing at university. They might be proportionally from more 'non-traditional' backgrounds than students from the more elite universities, but they are perceived as less vulnerable than the EY participants. These different discourses about the capacity to cope with failure and risk manifests in an interesting way across the two programmes. At SEU, it is the *person* who can fail (and therefore learn from the failure), whereas at EY, it is the *business* that can fail (leaving participants with no income). These different intonations of what constitutes failing are implicated in the perceived resilience of the participants to risk.

Discussion

This chapter has explored two technologies of governance. At SEU, failure is understood as individual and a normal part of learning. The SEU Enterprise Bootcamp uses technologies of the self to focus on developing a self-regulating individual who is resilient and willing to take on risk. In contrast, at EY, the training focuses on technologies of production, focusing on limiting risk through developing carefully thought-out business plans. We have used Foucault's notion of governmentality to understand how these two programmes conceive of their participants, and the importance of risk and failure for understanding initiatives that aim to increase enterprise activities.

In academic debates about the emergence of the 'risk society' (Beck, 1992a,b), discussions have evolved into whether risk reduces the significance of class and other social structures on determining individual opportunities. Whereas post-modernists such as Lyotard (1979) and Baudrillard (1988) have argued that structural analyses have become reduced in their usefulness, others argue that while class structures are more obscured, they remain persistent features of social life (Furlong and Cartmel, 2007). Beck (1992a,b) notes that one of the features of risk society is that individuals have unequal vulnerabilities to risk. Furlong and Cartmel argue that 'Individuals' skill in managing risk should be regarded as a significant resource' (2007: 2). In our two enterprise courses, the capacities and resources of the participants to cope with and manage risk starkly informs the approaches of the two interventions. SEU, whose participants have a safety net, are encouraged to become confident entrepreneurs who are ready to learn from failure. The EY participants are cautioned against ill thought-out plans and are given long-term support to ensure that they make sensible, reasoned choices. While both programmes may lend themselves to fulfilling economic policy goals of increasing entrepreneurial activities, the mindsets that are promoted by each have very different resonances.

What both interventions have in common, however, is their derivation from neoliberal discourses of individual responsibilization. Neither programme has direct input or funding from the state; it is still the individual young people in both cases who must accept the risks and deal with any failures. We have argued previously (Wilde and Leonard, 2018) that although the young people who participated in EY experienced very little material change in circumstances, those who continued with their businesses did gain satisfaction and the flexible working that had attracted them to self-employment in the first place. But their structural disadvantages remained, and enterprise, like many other labour market opportunities, is still largely governed by social structures such as class, race, gender and age. While enterprise may be lauded at EU, national and local policy levels as the saviour of flagging economies, the material benefits and rewards for the individuals who take on the risk of these activities remain to be seen.

FOUR

Internships in London

If the 'new precariat' is the major emerging class within post-industrial capitalist society (Standing, 2011), then the 'intern' has become a poster child for this class, conjuring up images of endless unpaid episodic labour, with the carrot of 'paid', gainful, and potentially, 'creative' work dangled as an elusive reward at the end of it. (Lee, 2015: 459)

Introduction

This chapter explores the growing use of internships as a route into certain careers of choice. Although internships have been common practice in a few professions since the 1960s, such placements, typically unpaid, burgeoned during the years of the 2008–12 recession, becoming a widespread strategy deployed both by organizations to enhance their workforce and young people keen to enhance their CVs with work experience at a time when paid jobs were in short supply. This chapter argues, however, that internships, particularly during the years of the 2008–12 economic crisis, are a highly exclusive entry route scheme, powerfully structured by social class. They vary considerably in terms of quality, and it is, in the main, only those young people with family resources who are able to access and benefit from the most prestigious internships.

The chapter begins with an overview of the bifurcated discourse of internships. On the one hand, they are positioned as a valuable means by which young people can access much-needed work experience to gain paid employment in a chosen career, but, on the other, they have come to be heavily critiqued as a highly exploitative means by which organizations enjoy talent for free. We then interrogate the policy landscape of internships, revealing this also to be a highly contested terrain that reflects the opposing discourses. Our case study of internships in London concentrates on a highly prestigious 'blue-chip' scheme accessed primarily by young, middle-class undergraduates from elite universities. This scheme is compared with the experiences of young people on other schemes that offer far less in terms of remuneration and work experience. Our research reveals that the young people with middle-class backgrounds enjoy contexts and institutions – such as family, their higher education institutions and the employing organization offering the internships – that 'helicopter' over their transitions. In contrast, for many young people from working-class backgrounds on other internship schemes, a 'no-rescue', 'hands-off' culture prevails. As a consequence, these young people need to take more individual-level responsibility for their career planning, labour market access and skills and training development.

The bifurcated discourse of internships: valuable experience or cynical exploitation?

Although internships became a hot topic in recession-fuelled debates about youth employability in the UK, they are not, in fact, a new phenomenon. In some professions, such as medicine, law and politics, they have existed for nearly a century, while in others, such as fashion, the media and the creative industries, they have been a regular feature for well over 50 years. However, over the past 20 years, the practice of interning – a period of unpaid or, occasionally, low-paid work experience, undertaken in an occupation of choice – has proliferated (Perlin, 2011). In the UK, internships mushroomed significantly during the 2008–12 economic recession, when they became widely adopted by a broad range of professions and industrial sectors as the principal point of entry into their white-collar worlds (Perlin, 2011). For graduates in particular, internships developed as a key governing technology by which a 'work-ready' subjectivity could be produced. During the height of the recession in 2010, an estimated one in five employers anticipated taking on interns (CIPD, 2010) and by 2017, up to 70,000 internships were performed, mostly by graduates (IPPR, 2017). Indeed, higher education policy sustains this upwards trajectory, with the Wilson review (2014) recommending all university students have access to workplace experience as part of the broader government agenda to upskill the British economy (GOV.UK, 2018a). As well as forming a common first step after graduation, undergraduates are now also increasingly expected to undertake an internship as an accredited component of their programme of study (O'Connor and Bodicoat, 2017), or 'voluntarily', on an individual basis, during vacations (Universities UK, 2002; Allen et al, 2013).

Yet while internships now constitute a significant and sustained restructuring of the UK's youth employment strategies, they are mired in political controversy. On the one hand touted as a key means of gaining the on-the-job *experience* and training viewed as essential by many employers before even considering recruitment (HEFCE, 2011; IPPR, 2017), on the other they are accused of cynically *exploiting* young people and reproducing inequalities, by being routinely unpaid and selecting predominantly through established social networks (Perlin, 2011; Social Mobility and Child Poverty Commission, 2014; IPPR, 2017; Grant-Smith and McDonald, 2018). Academic research and personal testimony have revealed how, most particularly in the cultural and creative industries, many interns suffer from poor-quality working conditions, receiving little in the way of remuneration, meaningful learning opportunities or workplace respect, and yet being no further forward in their attempts to secure a paid job in their sector of choice (Figiel, 2013; Frenette, 2013; Siebert and Wilson, 2013; Grant-Smith and McDonald, 2018). As internships have burgeoned, grass-roots activism, by campaigners such as Interns Aware, Internocracy and the Carrot Workers Collective, as well as intense scrutiny by the media, have exposed bad practice and raised awareness of the vulnerable positioning of interns (Grant-Smith and McDonald, 2018). A key issue of concern is the reliance on personal contacts and predominance of London in most internship positions, which results in an exclusive, class-based opportunity structure, most likely to benefit those young people with families with the correct contacts, living within commutable distance of the capital and who are wealthy enough to support them while they work unpaid (Allen et al, 2013; France and Roberts, 2017; Grant-Smith and McDonald, 2018). That internships play an active role in fundamentally challenging social mobility in the UK was recognized by the Panel on Fair Access to the Professions (Cabinet Office, 2012), which also concluded that a significant proportion did not provide high-quality work experience. A poll conducted by the Social Mobility Commission in 2017 revealed that most people in the UK support a legal ban on unpaid internships and unpaid work experience lasting more than four weeks (GOV.UK, 2017). The debate still chunters on, with the Unpaid Work Experience Prohibition Bill slowly making its way through the parliamentary process.

The bifurcation that pervades the internship discourse can, in part, be explained by the elasticity of the concept itself. The term is applied to highly diverse forms of work experience/employment, encompassing varied working conditions, benefits and rewards, occupational progressions and payment expectations, an ambiguity not helped by the fact that legal definitions remain contested (Lawton and Potter, 2010). Indeed, the vagueness of what exactly constitutes an internship is a key theme in the literature (Frenette, 2013; Corrigan, 2015; Grant-Smith and McDonald, 2018), leading Perlin (2011) to conceptualize them as a 'many-headed monster' (Leonard, 2013). To attempt to reduce the incertitude, attempts have been made to provide a schematic overview of typical characteristics (Pegg and Caddell, 2016): internships may be offered by for-profit or not-for-profit organizations, sometimes in connection to a formal education institution (Grant-Smith and McDonald, 2018), and are shaped by four key aspects:

- Length: internships tend to last for at least three months and can run to between six and twelve months.
- Time: interns usually work set hours comparable to a full-time, paid member of staff.
- Work expectations: interns are usually required to complete specified tasks and to work towards set goals or deadlines, with performance monitored and evaluated.
- Contribution: interns usually conduct work which would otherwise be done by another staff member, thus making a significant and valuable contribution to an organisation. (Lawton and Potter, 2010: 4–5)

Further clarification is provided by Guile and Lahiff (2013: 16), who posit that internships offer 'the development of sector/company-specific expertise, personal and professional identity and entrepreneurial flair'. This is achieved through 'the experience of working within interdisciplinary and professional teams and the development of an understanding of the responsibilities and demands of specific work roles' and 'the opportunity to explore and test out how ideas and knowledge gained from education are applied in practice and, crucially, generate new networks of associates and industry contacts' (Guile and Lahiff, 2013: 16). This also delivers clear benefits to the employer, for whom internships can offer a cheap, 'try before you buy' approach, a sort of extended job interview that may result in an offer of employment if the young intern performs as required.

Interpretations such as these illustrate how internships may operate as an important governing technology to produce the neoliberal subject. In the ways that they shift the responsibility for, and, often as not, costs of, early career training on to the individual young person, internships encapsulate the neoliberal shift from macro-level institutions to the micro-level of the individual. Forty years ago, training was predominantly perceived as an integral component of entry level jobs: 'graduate trainee schemes', for example, abounded in both the public and private sector, whereby it was the employer's responsibility to provide and/or fund an extended period of training in the first few years of a young person's employment. Internships demonstrate how such schemes have significantly diminished, with the identification, sourcing and costs of training and development transferred to the individual worker (Grant-Smith and McDonald, 2018). Thus while, on the face of it, the two versions of the internship discourse *appear* to offer paradoxical positions for young people, they both rest on shared assumptions of neoliberal governmentality: individualization, enterprise and the personal responsibilization of employability.

At the same time, however, as this chapter proceeds to demonstrate, the discursive field of internships is nuanced by the actual interventionist practices that are adopted at the organizational level. Our research reveals that differences in internship experiences are stark, according to who they are undertaken by and with which organization. This, in turn, results in huge diversity in the ways in which interns are positioned, and position themselves, within the broader neoliberal discourses of individualization, responsibilization and risk. This adds nuance, therefore, to the claims of Beck and Beck-Gernsheim (2002) and others who argue that the neoliberal agenda affects *all* young people as social structures decline in social force. Our research on internships underscores how neoliberalism, in practice, is experienced as a classed phenomenon that produces very different subject positions for young people through both family and organizational contexts. The young people in our study from middle-class backgrounds reveal a sense of embeddedness in contexts that are highly collectivist in nature, with family, higher education institute and the employing organization 'helicoptering' over their transitions. Indeed, there is little need, or even space, for individualized responsibility or decision making for this group. In contrast, a 'no-rescue', 'hands-off' culture prevails for many young people from working-class backgrounds, necessitating more personal and individual-level responsibility for their career planning, labour market access and skills and training development. Employing organizations located within these class sectors sustain inequalities in family and higher education institution capacity by providing far less support for their interns. In sum, the vast differences within internships means that they are, in themselves, an active means of class reproduction that route young people into un/employment, and adulthood, in fundamentally unequal ways.

Internships as policy: a contested terrain

The controversy surrounding internships grew as they developed as a key policy intervention for the UK's recession-hit graduate labour market. In 2009, the coalition government launched a £40 million fund for internships, supported by an Office for Graduate Opportunities (OGO) initiative to provide a one-stop shop through a website advertising thousands of placements, a high proportion of which were unpaid. The consensus at this time, by many policy makers and higher education institutions alike, was that doing *any* internship, even if unpaid, was a valuable means to employability (Allen et al, 2013; Pegg and Caddell, 2016). Since the recession, however, the policy terrain has shifted, particularly with regard to the issue of payment. While the OGO website is still operational, it now only advertises *paid* internships.

Simultaneous to 'the internship as good experience' policy discourse gaining traction, other policy makers began to express real concern about the supposed 'benefits' of internships to young people, as well as to the labour market and society more broadly. Most recently, *unpaid* internships have become a particular focus of policy, critiqued as exploitative and socially divisive. There are debates about the legality of unpaid internships (Walker, 2013), the morality of employers hiring without advertising and ignoring the minimum wage rule (Low Pay Commission, 2011; Montacute, 2018), and social mobility and inequality, in terms of who can afford to do internships and who benefits from them (Montacute, 2018). It is recognized that young people hoping to enter the media and creative industries, fashion, publishing, the charity sector and politics, where demand for jobs often exceeds supply, are particularly vulnerable (Frenette, 2013; Siebert and Wilson, 2013; Corrigan, 2015; Shade and Jacobson, 2015; Leonard et al, 2016). Not paying young people for productive work, which may be fee-earning and bring positive economic outcomes for an organization, is clearly exploitative (Grant-Smith and McDonald, 2016). While payment demonstrates a clear recognition of value produced, more critically, it contributes to the living expenses incurred when undertaking an internship. A key criticism of non-payment therefore is that it is a socially divisive technology, contributing to a 'new elitism' (Perlin, 2011) that embodies and sustains inequalities already produced through class, race and ethnicity, gender, education, personal/family wealth and connections and place differentials (Perlin, 2011; Coslett, 2015). Many internships are sourced through family connections (Siebert and Wilson, 2013) and based in London, where it is estimated that it will cost £1,019 a month to work unpaid, even assuming travel expenses are paid by the employer (Montacute, 2018). Clearly those from wealthy families, living in London, and with the right sort of social connections, are the winners here, with those from low-income, out-of-town families at a considerable disadvantage.

Unpaid internships can be exploitative in other ways too. Many interns, particularly in the cultural industries and the charity sector, invest much of themselves, their identities and their personal time in their work (Hesmondhalgh, 2010). From a post-Foucauldian perspective, we can see that highly competitive internships act as a form of governmentality, whereby individuals take action on themselves, to construct themselves in highly visible ways as just the kind of neoliberal, enterprising subject that employers reward with paid, secure work. This clearly benefits organizations, who may draw on interns' personal qualities and energy for productive purposes (Leonard et al, 2016; Illgner, 2018). However, the promise of a paid job may never materialize, and interns may be trapped in low-skill level jobs under-utilizing their skills (Green et al, 2016). Indeed, much of the anecdotal testimony written by interns reveals the mundane nature of their work, and lack of training and skills development that is often encountered (Figiel, 2013; Shade and Jacobson, 2015; Illgner, 2018). Non-standard employment conditions, such as no entitlement to holiday and sick pay for example, further increases workers' exposure to 'bad jobs' (Siebert and Wilson, 2013).

Policy makers legislating for payment have achieved some success (Butler, 2018), and now most internships pay at least the minimum wage. For those companies that do not, HM Revenue and Customs is now sending out 'warning letters', particularly targeting the media, performing arts, and law and accountancy firms with a poor reputation of employing interns on an unpaid basis. The business minister, Andrew Griffiths, has maintained: 'Employing unpaid interns as workers to avoid paying the national minimum wage is against the law and exploitative. No one should feel like they have to work for free to get the skills and experience they need to get ahead' (quoted in Butler, 2018). In some contradiction to these sentiments, however, the Conservative Party of which Griffiths is a member, is simultaneously still advertising for unpaid internships (Lee, 2018).

In sum, the problem, as it is predominantly conceptualized in policy terms, is not that internships per se should be abolished, but that the working conditions under which they are currently performed should be improved. Interventions such as widening advertising strategies, or payment for more than four weeks' work, are designed to extend the reach of internships as a form of governmentality, whereby more young people participate, rather than providing more structured forms of support. As such, policy is doing little to address the fundamental social structural constraints that prevent less advantaged young people from accessing and undertaking high- quality internships.

It was against this highly contested landscape that our empirical research was conducted. While existing research on the experiences of young people performing internships remains somewhat sketchy and unsystematic (Leonard, 2013), it is important to acknowledge that some organizations *do* provide highly valued and well-structured training schemes that are well paid and offer good working conditions (Paisey and Paisey, 2010; Thompson, 2011; Maelah et al, 2014. These 'blue-chip' schemes provide clear occupational learning outcomes and career benefits for young people (Donnan and Carthy, 2011; Maelah et al, 2014), and as such are sought after as a future-oriented, 'braggable investment' (Corrigan, 2015: 341). Usually offered by the top graduate recruiters in sectors such as finance, accounting and consultancy, their numbers have consistently risen each year since 2010, by as much as 50 per cent according to a report by the Institute for Public Policy Research (IPPR, 2017). Nearly half of these employers now admit that applicants to their organizations who have not gained experience through an internship, often while doing their degree, will 'have little or no chance of receiving a job offer', regardless of academic qualifications (IPPR, 2017: 3).

The regional imbalances in the UK economy that concentrate jobs in London and the South East mean that most internship opportunities are based in the capital, and certainly those high-quality schemes that provide access to the elite professions. Finance and banking, the law and politics, as well as the creative industries and the third sector, are especially geographically restricted, with up to 85 per cent of all their internships in the Greater London region (IPPR, 2017). For this reason, we chose to base our research on internships in London, aiming to encompass interning experiences in a range of industrial sectors. It is to this we now turn.

Case study: internships in London: 'helicoptering' or 'no rescue'?

On the one hand, therefore, we were interested in exploring an example of a 'blue-chip' internship scheme: highly selective and prestigious, with a likelihood of good employment conditions and outcomes. To this end, we gained access to undertake ethnographic research at one of the prestigious 'Big Four'[1] professional services corporations, Global Accountants (GA), which is well known for its targeted recruitment strategies, particularly aimed at undergraduates (Bright Network, nd). On the other hand, we accessed a sample of young people who had interned in sports, the third sector and the digital industries.

Like many large organizations, GA has a range of entry routes for new recruits hoping to build a career here. Visiting GA in its glass-walled tower in the City of London, we chatted to Neil, Head of Student Recruitment. Neil explains that GA offers three primary intake groups: higher apprentices, in the main school leavers; the traditional graduate route, whereby graduates joining straight from university with a degree; and the new, employer-led degree route, whereby students apply for what is called the Flying Start Degree at one of a small number of specific universities. This is a four-year undergraduate programme

---

[1] The generic term encompassing the four biggest professional service networks in the world, specializing in a range of corporate finance, management consultancy, legal and tax services.

in which a year's work experience is embedded during the degree. The aim is to support wider access into the accountancy profession, by paying students as they study towards a degree while also undertaking work placements with the firm. This is innovative, enabling some young people to accumulate human and social capital they might otherwise not have access too.

Also much changed is the traditional graduate entry route. Once applicants waited until they had graduated before starting employment at GA, but now, according to Neil:

> '... the last six or seven years have transformed the way that people access these opportunities, so 20 per cent of the jobs we bring in through the graduate route will be people who we have identified from first year onwards. So Internships have always been popular, you know, but they've grown very significantly as a route into jobs.'

Internships have therefore emerged as an extension to the traditional scheme, a pre-graduation stage that opens up opportunities to undergraduates to commence their career-building strategies right from the start of their degree programmes. Although we interviewed Neil in 2014, the economic recession was not mentioned as a driver for the rise in the numbers of their internships. To the contrary, GA is aware that they are operating in a highly competitive market, wherein those with the 'right skills and qualifications' may be able, in accountancy, to 'call the shots' in terms of employment options. Neil explains that this has created "a kind of new battle front in the war for talent" and GA's strategy is an attempt to lock 'talent' down early. It is clear that GA is looking for a certain 'type' of young person: someone seen to have an entrepreneurial mindset to start thinking about their future career early and willing to trade university vacations for work experience. GA then appoints those who have already conducted an internship to become 'brand ambassadors', visibly embodying and performing the role of someone who is 'employable' by GA. The role of the brand ambassador is to scout for talent and encourage other students to apply for an internship from their very first summer vacation through such strategies as stalls at Freshers' Fairs and "handing out sweets on Valentine's Day", as Anna, one of our interviewees, put it.

Despite the need to attract talent, elite professional service firms in the UK are highly socially exclusive, with new entrants likely to be from relatively privileged socioeconomic backgrounds (Ashley and Empson, 2016). The long-standing legacy of exclusionary hiring practices is being increasingly acknowledged by the sector, which is starting to make noises about the 'business case' for change (Ashley and Empson, 2013). For example, Neil explained that his role involved:

> '... building the team and the function that delivers on this, both in terms of making sure that we get the talent we need and that we, kind of, are addressing diversity within that and inclusion within that roughly ... you know, the traditional ethnic, gender type of perspectives, and increasingly, you know, social mobility as well. That's it in a nutshell.'

In the face of this aim, Neil admits that "the market isn't fully aware of [our] agnosticism" towards university and degree. This lack of awareness is perhaps with good reason: it is still the case that "the highest number of people we recruit are from the likes of Durham, Manchester, Warwick, Bristol", all ranked in the top 20 of British universities. A widening participation strategy is in place, which is "to broaden the message through a lighter touch approach to a much wider range of universities". Neil acknowledges that this is still only 30-odd, rather than the 125 or so that GA could, in theory, recruit from. In addition, GA is attempting to access "the best of the students at the universities further down the league tables through partnerships", who are then offered mentoring and master classes. The company has also launched a "corporate quality piece of e-learning, a tutorial effectively, for interviewees. It's an open source, on the website, anyone can look at it". It is taking a more nuanced approach to correlating academic credentials to "who might make a good accountant". Neil admits that "whilst we are hiring people through these routes, we are not hiring as many as we knew would be representative of that market"; 60 per cent of the intake is privately educated. A clear gap remains, therefore, between the (admittedly rather lukewarm) rhetoric around diversity and widening participation and recruitment in practice.

The class-based nature of GA's recruitment strategies was reflected in our ethnography. This included participation in the Talent Academy, the final, residential stage of the selection process, as well as in-depth, follow-up interviews with 11 successful applicants who had secured internships, either in the current round or in the past. In addition, we interviewed a range of relevant key informants, such as Neil, who were all involved in GA's 'early identification of talent' (EIT) recruitment team. At the residential event, the first activity was 'speed networking', where all the (131) applicants gathered, giving us a chance to view their demography. We noticed that there were slightly more male than female participants; the majority were White, with quite a few Asian, a couple of Middle Eastern, and a handful of White international students, but no Black interns. Most of the accents were southern England and 'posh', although voices from the Midlands and the North could also be heard. The classed and gendered nature of the intake did not go unnoticed by some of the interns. Anna, a geography undergraduate at Bristol, summarized that "there's definitely a demographic that the interns that I was working with fit into, sort of quite 'middle class male' ... it's sort of historically a male profession that boys tend to apply [for] more than girls".

Among our interviewees all, bar one, were from what Neil had termed 'upper tier' universities – Glasgow, London,

Bristol, Durham, Exeter, Manchester, Sheffield – with only Andy having attended a 'new' university' in the Midlands. When asked, most of this group self-identified as middle class: they talked about attending prep school, private school or boarding school and described professional family backgrounds:

> 'Both my parents went to university, and one of my grandparents went to university as well, so I'd probably say that puts us in middle class.' (Evie)

Tanvi was an exception: her father is a courier and her mother 'works in an office'. She was the first in her family to attend university.

Several mentioned having parents who also worked for GA or one of the other Big Four, and it was often a mix of both family and university support that instigated the application for an internship with GA for most of our interviewees. Indeed, many had been influenced or prompted to apply by family members who were either already working in the sector or, in the case of siblings, had done the internship themselves and profited from it:

> 'Both my parents did work for GA. My sister did one [an internship] so I knew about it through her, and then because she had done one I think the expectation was that I would do one … She loved it, she met loads of people but she was working really long hours, so I think I've got expectations from her that it will be very hard work. Which is a good thing to go in with expectations like that, like I don't think I'll be sort of surprised by how much work they give me.' (Anna)

GA's selection process to the internship programme is rigorous, but the prizes are clear: the interns are paid well, the same as a new member of staff and, unless something goes very wrong, are usually offered a job on completion of their degree. Typically, around 8,000 undergraduates apply for one of 300 places, most often during their second year at university, progressing through a stringent, multi-stage process that consists of an online questionnaire, attendance at an assessment centre and a telephone interview. They then attend a final two-/three-day residential course conducted in a smart country hotel, just north of London, with its own golf course, gym and swimming pool. Celia, an EIT assessor, explains:

> 'This is the final hurdle for the interns. They have done all the assessments that a new starter would, this is the last bit before they get on to the graduate placement. They have to be professional, have the right attitude and prove themselves. It's about how they come across now.'

During the residential, the would-be interns are introduced to various 'real projects' that they could be working on during the internship. Celia informs us that this is what differentiates GA internships: the interns are involved in 'real' work and given the appropriate technical training in their chosen line of service: assurance, tax, deals or consulting. This starts straight away at the residential event, where the interns learn "lots of crucial stuff and they love it, that training is why they are here" (Celia). This initial training, however, is less technical and more focused on developing the self. Clear use is made of technologies of the self, by which the young people are informed how to construct themselves as 'employable' by GA. The key session of their first morning is to hear from Lewis, a current partner, who, after talking through his career journey, moves on to talking about the identity of the firm. The values Lewis explains are intimately connected to discourses of neoliberalism: GA aims to be iconic: a powerhouse in the sector. It has ambition and aims to be front of mind in professional services. It has vision and does the right thing for its clients, its people, and its community. As Lewis adds that these are the behaviours that employees should adopt, both collectively and individually: the neoliberal foundations of GA's technologies of governance are made clear. GA positions its interns within a set of subjectivities by which GA hopes to represent the organization: quality; do the right thing; ethical capitalism; trust; integrity; balance; morality; dependability; relevance; principled. Those that perform this version of the self appropriately are clearly well rewarded: "What is the best thing about GA?" one of the interns asks. "The personal development and professional support," Lewis confirms:

> 'The support from the firm was brilliant, fantastic; it's miles apart, [when I moved] they put me up in temporary accommodation near the office while we looked for somewhere permanent, so I could be near to my wife and son. Regardless of what grade you are, there is loads of support for that sort of thing.'

Lewis's session is swiftly followed with another on "behaviours, and what we expect from you". Entitled You as a Professional, the young people are informed that GA employees are expected to demonstrate five core attributes: relationships; business acumen; technical capabilities; global acumen; and whole leadership. They should be 'authentic' and 'inclusive' leaders, who inspire others:

> 'You love making a difference wherever you can, using your top technical abilities and brilliant business acumen. Your mind-set is global, going beyond borders, and you know how to build meaningful relationships. We're all different, but we're all GA Professionals: all leaders. And we're stronger together.' (GA video)

The governance of expected behaviours extends to how the interns should look: they are told that while dinner is casual the first night, for the second night they should dress in business wear for the partner dinner. While the session ends with the advice that interns should "take control of their careers", it is clear that, if this is to be with GA, a narrow range of neoliberal performances are valorized. The next presentations, given by a couple of ex-interns, confirm this. Giles, who now works in accountancy, embodies enthusiasm:

'I really like working here! I'm enjoying it so much, it's flexible, you can devise your own career path, in an environment of like-minded people, in an industry I want to work in. Make really useful contacts! People are ambitious, but they want to see others do well too. Here's some pictures of me at the summer ball! My advice would be to build your networks, and this starts today.'

The internship, Giles explains, is a fabulous opportunity, offering

'an intensive example of what it's like to work here: genuine objectives and full appraisal cycle, they treat you like a fully-fledged employee. To have the job offer in your final year, it's great to have the pressure off, to have that security. The challenges of learning, learning about GA, the tangible sense of day to day work which you only get by doing it.'

Giles is right: the sense of security the job offer brings emerged as a key attraction for our respondents. Anna explains that this made it

'… definitely the best route for me from a security point of view. Like I like to sort of have all my ducks lined up! My sister did a banking internship and then went into consultancy, and I know lots of other people who have done this sort of placement at uni and that's been their way in.'

Evie, a management student at Exeter, agrees. She interned at the end of her second year and was then offered a job on graduation. Now employed full-time, and reflecting back on her internship, she explains:

'The peace of mind that it gave me in my final year was just so helpful, to just concentrate on work and nothing else. I just saw the stress that my housemates were going through trying to find jobs, and I don't think I would have done as well in my degree if I'd had the stress of finding a job and going to interviews as well. That probably was the main one for me, yeah knowing that you've got a job is so good, especially when it was a year ago, it's so much more difficult for graduates to find jobs, and you were hearing horror stories of people's brothers and sisters who have graduated a couple of years before who still were like working in Tesco because they couldn't find anything.'

An appreciation of 'security' was obviously one of the characteristics that GA clustered within its particular version of 'employability'. Security at this early stage would not attract every young undergraduate, however, some of whom may be keener to taste a range of options rather than tie themselves down even before graduation.

As well as the prospect of job security, the breadth of the training and wide-ranging experience was also cited as highly positive:

'It really kind of gave me a chance to experience lots of different industries ... it was a really good introduction to that world and gave the commercial awareness that they always talk about. It was very like hands-on I would say, most of my time was chargeable, so I was doing like real life work. And yeah like playing, I guess, like a relatively important part for an intern.' (Henrietta, studying Chinese and Economics, University of London)

The support system is strong, providing interns with both a buddy and a mentor. They are invited to frame objectives and then given the training to achieve these:

'We were all given a buddy who got in touch with me before I joined, so she kind of just introduced herself and was always ... there for me one on one basically and I sat with her for most of the time. And she'd find me work: there was always someone there to support you. And we were also given a People Manager – more formal, making sure everything's alright, if I had any concerns about the job and that sort of thing. So yeah it was one informal person that you could talk to about anything, and then one that was more about career development and that sort of thing, which was really good. And the whole team made like a real big effort as well. So everyone was really keen to have us, so the support system was really good, really good.' (Tanvi, ex-intern, studied Philosophy and Psychology, University of Sheffield)

It was clear that many of the interns had gained in professional development, as Henrietta summarizes nicely:

'Technically my computer skills are far, far better, even after six weeks. The business commercial awareness, that's greatly improved as well. Just even knowing like how firms work and how all the different sections fit together, it's really hard to understand that until you actually get in and see how it works. Communication skills, like that was really good, to be able to practise those. Presentation skills. And just generally like confident I think, the fact that everyone is so approachable – even Partners – just to have the confidence to walk into an office and say "do you have ten minutes" and, you know, 99 per cent of the time they'll say "yeah of course, sit down", so the door's open, they have time to see you. So yeah I think the whole communication, networking, and meeting as many people as possible, these past six weeks have really … I've definitely sort of changed myself because I would have never really felt comfortable doing that sort of thing before.'

Lingering in some accounts, however, was the possibility that security and support came at the cost of any real interest in the work itself. Anna admitted that "for the most part it's quite an inoffensive internship, you know the hours are fine, the work was boring but it wasn't impossible". After some hesitation, she continues:

'If they do offer me the job I think I'll take it just … worst comes to worst I'll train for three years, get a really useful qualification, find out what else I want to do. There's nothing else that's calling to me more currently. I won't say it's my lifelong dream to be an accountant, but there's nothing else that actually is my lifelong dream, so I'm just being practical.'

In stark contrast were the experiences of those undergraduates we talked to who had independently secured internships with a range of smaller organizations within the private and voluntary sector. These included a sports science student who interned at a football club, and several international economics and computer science students from China who had interned at Chinese fintech organizations. While these internships were also highly competitive, they varied in quality, and were clearly experienced in much more negative terms by the young people. None of the respondents felt that their internship offered them much in the way of training or support for future career development. Access was the first major hurdle, but rather than having a clear application process, these internships were secured by the young people 'cold calling' and offering their services. For the Chinese students, however, it was clear that personal networks, or *guanxi*, were essential for 'getting in'. A second contrast was the fact that these internships were unpaid. While some we talked to did have some family resources to draw on to support themselves, others had to work double shifts to supplement their incomes.

George, a sports graduate from a minor college in the suburbs of London, spent a year on short-term internships and applications before being finally accepted on to a year-long internship at Greenboots Football Club. This internship, at a semi-professional club, was highly competitive and the experience was vital if George was to have any chance of finding paid work within the sports sector:

'I'd chosen this internship because by this point I'd been looking for a year, and although I don't like football I thought "I've got to get something on my CV" otherwise there's going to be a very big gap and it looks suspicious to an employer.'

The standard practice in the sector is that internships are unpaid, not even offering reimbursement for expenses. George was fortunate that he was able to live at home, but his family circumstances meant that he also had to work part-time in a bar to sustain himself. As well as funding his degree, he had also paid for himself to undertake a coaching qualification, train as a cycle mechanic and gain membership of a professional body. Yet while George clearly exemplifies the neoliberal self, and in many ways, given his sense of drive and personal responsibility, in stronger terms than the interns at GA, this technology of the self was not rewarded by the organization. He explained that interns were given little in the way of training and ongoing support, and that the content of the work was dull and failed to utilize their skills, qualifications and experience:

> 'It almost felt like they weren't trusting us to use the knowledge we had, so as if we didn't have the knowledge and experience in order to do the job ... if we were asked to do something which was approaching something you could do, if we didn't understand them perfectly and do it exactly the way they wanted it, the way they'd then respond to that was quite negative. So ... the environment I didn't like at all. It felt like we were often doing a lot of jobs that they could do if they worked a longer day, like putting equipment away or taking it out, and I think it was almost doing the job they didn't want to. So yeah, the tasks were very menial ... there wasn't an opportunity to actually learn by asking and suggesting "what if we did it this way?" because there was a very fixed idea of what they had to do and what they wanted to do, and we weren't given a chance to have any input into that.'

Clearly, the football club did not value autonomy and a sense of responsibility as a technology of the self. The fact that George was given such poor-quality work contrasted with the bar work he was doing to fund the internship:

> 'I spent most of my time being the water boy! Being the water boy. I thought "I did not go through three years of a degree to fill up water bottles". And I got to realize that most of my tasks were making drinks, either the water bottles or the protein shakes, and cleaning or tidying the gym. At the time I was working two or three days in a

local pub, so I was doing the same thing except I was getting minimum wage for it. And in the pub, although I didn't like it at first, eventually it got to a point where I felt like I was trusted to get on with it, whereas I never felt that on the internship ... it was more micro managed than it should be in certain ways and less in others where it should have been.'

In the end, George decided to cut his losses:

'I actually didn't feel like I was getting as much out of the agreement as they were, so I just thought ... I decided to cut my losses and leave.'

Chen, a high-performing computer scientist with outstanding academic credentials, was also hugely disappointed by the quality of his internship in a Chinese telecommunications company in London, where his technical skills were under-utilized. He remarked that "some of my friends also got internships ... I knew someone who worked for JP Morgan, another with HSBC and Barclays. So, I compare my situation with their situations, and I find, oh totally different!". While Chen's *guanxi* – his Chinese-based social and cultural connections – had secured his internship within the Chinese-owned and managed organization, he did not have the right networks to get into the banks that his (British) friends had accessed. He enjoyed none of the benefits that they, or the interns at GA, received. Like George, a key problem for Chen was a lack of autonomy and pay: "I am not very free during my internship and I received no payment". As a consequence, he had to pay for himself to live in Whitechapel, but was fortunate that his parents had sufficient financial capital to send him money from China. In contrast to the experiences of those at GA, where the support, training and good rates of pay to some extent compensated for any boredom experienced in the work, Chen was unhappy with his experience:

> 'My director controlled me totally. I am not interested in the work, this is a telecom company and I have studied the network, but I don't like this job, I don't like this job. I feel really bored during the daytime ... I was asked to do nothing, just search on the internet, you can imagine how difficult, how boring it is. So I just spend one week doing that or doing nothing. I'm really enthusiastic to learn, to do more challenging things. But I can't.'

Chen also decided to quit, having received nothing in the way of training. He managed to secure another paid internship, also in a Chinese company, although he would have preferred to work in "Western companies, this is what I really want to get". However Chen's internalization of the governing of the self means that he recognizes that he may not possess the required social and cultural capital:

> 'I think I'm not very ... I met some students from Cambridge and from Oxford, they worked in those big companies, and I think well, except the university is different, the abilities are the same. But I think some big companies in London, they have the ability to say, "we'll only take people from Oxford".'

While George and Chen's experiences were the poorest among the interns we talked to, none of the non-GA interns enjoyed the sort of training, pay and employment outcomes enjoyed by the interns at GA. As we now go on to discuss, this highlights important diversities within internship schemes and the significantly different positions taken by organizations within broader discourses of neoliberalism.

Discussion

Concerns about the vast diversity in the quality of internships in the UK are exacerbated by the socially unequal nature of young people's encounters with them. The better the quality of the internship, the more likely it is to be occupied by someone from a privileged family and educational background. In the blue-chip programmes, most often accessed through the possession of the 'right' mix of UK-based social and cultural capital, young people are embedded in a multifaceted support network that governs their transition from education to work. Within this, the organization adds to the family and university advantages that 'helicopter' over the individual young person, ensuring smoothness of progression from the one stage to the next. Although the young interns we spoke to in this position often used the language of agency in the expression of their choices, their levels of individual responsibility for, and risks within, their transitions to stable, paid work are low. There are multiple other agents in their lives, actively supporting the seamlessness of their transfer between education and work. Indeed, in some respects, these high-quality internships function to blur the transition from the 'education stage' to the 'work stage', overlaying the former with the latter. This intertwining of at least these two systems of governance – if not more, if family and social background are included – means that the lives of these young people are heavily governed. For the organization, the internship serves as a technology through which work tasks, workplace behaviour and performance are all subject to high levels of surveillance and control. Managed by objectives, individual performances are measured, and results fed back in order that interns may seek to improve. In this way, organizational goals are transformed into personal goals and self-control supplemented, or replaced, by organizational control (McKinlay and Starkey, 1998).

In contrast, many young people, often those without the relevant capital, experience internships that offer little in the way of support for career development and the transition to good-quality, paid work in a desired career. There is clear diversity by sector, with organizations within, for example, the sports and leisure, creative and digital industries, which are often over-supplied with keen young applicants hoping to access careers, using this advantage to avoid proper oversight of training, good-quality work tasks and payment and other benefits essential to independent living. This group of young people are in a position of 'no rescue': positioned within policy discourse as responsible for their own careers, they are left unsupported within their organizational contexts. In the diversities of internship quality, organizational 'governance' becomes in itself productive of hierarchy and inequality. While on the one hand, therefore, 'good internships' may mean more surveillance and control, and a loss of personal autonomy, this 'middle-class problem' is an enabler of good-quality training and workplace experience, and the support to develop the sorts of neoliberal behaviours desired by employers.

FIVE

Volunteering in Glasgow, Scotland

Introduction

This chapter turns to investigate volunteering, much vaunted in recent years as a valuable means by which young people may gain valuable experience for work and careers. The 2008–12 economic recession fuelled this discourse more powerfully, and it became mainstreamed into government advice to young people struggling to access jobs. As such, the distinction between traditional understandings of volunteering as an altruistic activity and volunteering as working unpaid has become rather messily blurred. Volunteering has thus emerged as a powerful technology by which to govern young people, not only to become individually accountable for their work futures, but to develop a range of other 'responsible' performances and subjectivities associated with active citizenship.

This chapter commences with a discussion of the discursive shift in youth volunteering that has transformed traditional conceptualizations of volunteering as a performance of active citizenship to seeing the activity in more instrumental terms. We then analyze the policy context, to argue that policies to encourage more youth volunteering are based on a conundrum: the fact that there is no robust evidence to support the view that volunteering *is* a beneficial means by which to access paid employment. Our case study of a volunteering organization in Scotland that delivers bespoke employability training to young people and includes daily spells of volunteering in a range of voluntary sector workplaces provides some insight into why this might be the case. A lack of interest in young people's development by some of the managers in work experience placements can lead to the young people 'time filling' with meaningless, poor-quality work. Further, the lack of engagement by private sector employers makes it difficult for young people to gain experience in organizations offering paid employment opportunities. It is important to recognize, however, that paid employment is not an appropriate outcome for every young person. Our research also underscores the significant contribution of trainers to other beneficial outcomes of volunteering programmes, such as the confidence and wellbeing of young trainees. For some, the enhanced levels of self-worth which the programme delivered was a success in its own right.

From active citizenship to responsible employability: the discursive shift in youth volunteering

Since well before the turn of this century, successive British governments have made extensive efforts to encourage volunteering by young people. However, over the course of this period, a number of discursive shifts have taken place in terms of the policy benefits volunteering is claimed to deliver. The 1980s ushered in several programmes that connected youth volunteering with employability (Ockenden and Hill, 2009; Kamerāde and Ellis Paine, 2014), but, during the late 1990s, as unemployment levels dropped, there was a powerful shift towards volunteering's social and civic associations and adjudged individual benefits (Rochester et al, 2010). Volunteering became primarily promulgated as a key remedy for perceived declines in civil society and social cohesion, and, particularly in relation to young people, growing disaffection and alienation (Gaskin, 2004). As the 21st century progressed, a more positive assessment of youth culture emerged, emphasizing young people's greater sense of tolerance, concern with social justice and engagement with a wide range of political causes such as environmentalism, feminism and anti-consumerism (Brooks, 2009; Manning, 2010).

Within this broad discourse of volunteering as 'active citizenship' (Brooks, 2007), the activity was predominantly understood in traditional terms, aligning with Davis Smith's (Davis Smith with Howlett, 2003) definition of volunteering as being constituted by three core elements: freely undertaken, of benefit to others, and unpaid. Volunteering was seen as a means to enable young people to 'reconnect' politically as citizens (Lister et al, 2002), engage with local communities and minimize the uncertainties produced through an increasingly individualized society (Hustinx, 2001; Beck and Beck-Gernsheim, 2002). The government-appointed Russell Commission proclaimed: 'Society as a whole will benefit as young people express themselves as active citizens' (Russell Commission, 2005: 6). Thus, while the importance of gaining skills, experience, qualifications and references were all acknowledged as motivations for young people's volunteering, it was altruistic reasons, such as concern for social issues, mutual support and even having fun, that were framed as key incentives (Gaskin, 2004).

After the onset of the economic crisis in 2008, a shift occurred in policy discourses on youth volunteering. As young people from across the social and educational spectrum faced mounting levels of youth unemployment (Bell and Blanchflower, 2010; 2012; Heinz, 2014), volunteering came to be positioned in more instrumental terms, with the 'unpaid *work*' connotation the most emphasized (Dean, 2014). The dominant discourse now, as in the 1980s, was employability. In its rebooted construction, young people's subjectivities were framed through notions of individualism, responsibilization and 'work readiness' (Dean, 2013, 2014). Increasingly, volunteering was promulgated by, first, the Labour and then the coalition government, as an effective strategy to enhance employability skills and the chance of accessing paid work (Brooks, 2007; Holdsworth and Quinn, 2010; Anderson and Green, 2012). A raft of initiatives was introduced by the two governments, kicked off by the £8 million Volunteer Brokerage Scheme launched by the Department for Work and Pensions (DWP) in 2009 (DWP Welfare to Work and Equality Group, 2009), whereby the volunteering service was deployed to match benefits claimants' job-related interests and skills with volunteering placements. These would be 'short term and work focused, designed to enhance customer skills and boost a customer's CV' (DWP Welfare to Work and Equality Group, 2009: 3). This was joined by other schemes more specifically aimed at young people, such as vinvolved (the National Young Volunteers Service), the National Citizen Service, and Work Together, which aimed to encourage all young people 'to consider volunteering as a way of improving their employment prospects while looking for work' (DWP, 2012: 1). Volunteering burgeoned within higher education policy too, with undergraduates urged to improve their CVs and career prospects by volunteering (Brooks, 2007; Holdsworth and Quinn, 2010; Anderson and Green, 2012; Dean, 2015).

A proliferation of unpaid work programmes followed from 2011 onwards, promoted as encouraging out-of-work young people to gain experience of the labour market . These included the Work Experience Scheme for Job Seekers Allowance and the Graduate Talent Pool Internships (Mellors-Bourne and Day, 2011). At the same time, as discussed in Chapter Four, the 2008–12 recession and a shortage of paid jobs for young people fuelled an upsurge in unpaid work 'opportunities' more generally. As young people were exhorted to work unpaid to gain valuable work experience, and employers realized that they could access valuable talent for free, unpaid work schemes expanded across all industrial sectors.

Yet while sometimes blurred in policy discourses in more recent times, a distinction between 'volunteering' and 'unpaid work' nevertheless lingers in both research and common understanding. Volunteering is still, in many people's minds, predominantly associated with charitable contexts, and a host of empirical research is consistently drawn on to demonstrate that engagement with this sector is variously linked with a whole host of associated positive outcomes beyond employability skills, such as reduced incidence of 'problem' behaviours, improved wellbeing, higher self-confidence, a greater sense of community, increased levels of citizenship and continued participation in voluntary and political activity in later life (see Bennet and Parameshwaran, 2013). While employability is now increasingly perceived in policy discourses to overshadow these more traditional understandings of 'volunteering', these do not disappear altogether. Rather, they interplay to produce multiple meanings, which shift over time to serve a range of power interests, both civic and economic. As such, 'volunteering' forms a powerful neoliberal technology by which to govern young people, not only to become individually accountable for their work futures, but to develop a range of other 'responsible' performances and subjectivities (Holdsworth and Quinn, 2010; Nenga, 2012; Dean, 2013).

Bringing the voluntary sector into the youth employability policy agenda: context and conundrum

Through the DWP's Volunteer Brokerage Scheme (VBS), which aimed to get 42,000 volunteers of all ages into work, Volunteer Centres were encouraged not only to provide participants with work experience through volunteering, but also to bid for funding to establish local employability training programmes, particularly for people from disadvantaged social and educational backgrounds who are less likely to become involved with volunteering (Low et al, 2007; Ockenden and Hill, 2009; Mohan and Bulloch, 2012; Kamerāde and Ellis Paine, 2014). While the VBS applied to the Volunteer Centre network in England, Scotland also had an established network of Volunteer Centres and, as we go on to discuss, a sister scheme was also introduced here. The VBS was followed by further initiatives, such as the Volunteering for Stronger Communities project, funded by the Big Lottery from 2011–13, which also aimed to engage 'hard to reach' job seekers, and the DWP's Work Together scheme, which commenced in 2011. Ten years on, Volunteer Centres are now well established across the UK as key deliverers of employability training to the unemployed of all ages and social backgrounds, but especially disenfranchised young people.

The delegation of employability and skills training is part of the government's broader neoliberal agenda of 'rolling back' welfare provision, which is perceived as interfering with the workings of the market (Graeber, 2009). Consequently, a combination of market-based institutions and third sector organizations have stepped in to fill the void (Peck and Theodore, 2001; Gledhill, 2004; Wilde, 2016), not least within work and employability services. Frequently positioned by government as alternative in ethos and approach to traditional education and training centres, such as schools and further education colleges, Volunteer Centres are viewed as being in a good position to reach out to a wide variety of young people, including providing training to those who have been disaffected by conventional educational methods (Thompson, 2011; Newton et al, 2011). How successful are such schemes for enabling young people to access work? Further, is this good-quality work, the sort of work the young people may want to do in the long term and perhaps build a career within? While research investigating the link between volunteering and securing paid work has been somewhat scant, the studies that do exist reveal a far from straightforward picture, particularly for young people. The evidence suggests that volunteering not only has an unpredictable relationship with paid work, but may even produce a negative effect (Wilson, 2000; Ockenden and Hill, 2009; Ellis Paine et al, 2013; Kamerāde and Ellis Paine, 2014).

Where a positive relationship has been reported, volunteering has been conducted in specific contexts such as conservation and volunteering overseas, or has relied on a small sample and/ or self-report measures of impact (Newton et al, 2011; Ellis Paine et al, 2013). Ellis Paine and colleagues' study (2013), using the British Household Panel Survey, found a weak effect of volunteering on 'getting in' to employment for young people and, in terms of 'getting on', a negative effect on wage levels. These findings were confirmed by our own analysis using the Citizen Education Longitudinal Survey dataset, which finds that while undertaking voluntary activity may deliver some skills-related benefits, securing firm access to a paid career of choice was not one of them. All in all, as Ellis Paine and colleagues (2013: 369) conclude, we are left 'with a bit of a puzzle'. It was thus to contribute to the unravelling of the puzzle of whether volunteering is an effective method of gaining paid employment that we undertook a case study at a Volunteering Centre in Glasgow, Scotland.

Employability and volunteering interventions in Glasgow

Glasgow was selected as a region that both faced real challenges in youth unemployment and had prioritized volunteering as a key strategy to tackle this. Our key informant interviews with the Scottish Government, Skills Development Scotland, Jobcentre Plus and Glasgow City Council revealed that, over the past 50 years, Glasgow's employment opportunities for young people have suffered enormously: first pummelled by the industrial decline of its heavy industries, and then sustained by the detrimental impact of cyclical recessions. The hosting of the Commonwealth Games in 2014 was hugely welcome, seen to offer Glasgow a real opportunity to stem the tidal wave of unemployment threatened by the most recent 2008–12 economic crisis. A key intervention adopted by the city council therefore was to establish a range of Commonwealth

Employment Initiatives, which aimed to ensure that the new employment generated by the Commonwealth Games would provide a sustainable legacy for Glasgow's young people. Policies were rooted in place:

'So, there's two sides to it. One is that we're trying to create new employment opportunities, and then trying to make sure that Glasgow's young people are getting access to those. So, we make no bones about the fact that if you don't live in Glasgow you can't access this. So you have to be a Glasgow resident, and that's something that we check before we would register anybody on the system.' (Shirley, Youth Employment Manager, Glasgow City Council)

That Glasgow had a very specific set of localized youth employability issues was well recognized across our key informants. As Michael, a member of the Employment Skills Division at the Scottish Government, explained:

'In government there's always an issue about *local* delivery and consistency … because the needs in Aberdeen, for example, are not the same as the needs here as far as we're concerned, so it would be inappropriate to offer schemes that gave lots of money to employers in Aberdeen who don't need them, whereas here they do.'

Of concern to local policy makers is the fact that employers seem to have a perception that Glasgow's young people are less attractive a prospect than young people from other areas of Scotland. Shirley elucidates:

'Why don't they employ Glasgow young people? Because obviously Glasgow's the centre of a wider metropolitan area and our sense is that a young person from other local authority areas is more likely to get that employment than a Glasgow young person. And a part of that is because Glasgow's education system is seen to be poorer and so young people are better in some of the other areas ... why have they got that perception – because it's not a real reflection? ... They were saying "oh but we can we not take kids from East Dunbartonshire" or whatever, and we're saying "no, if you want our money, they've got to be our kids ...", "ah but the Glasgow kids are useless". And it's like, "OK well give us a chance".'

Differences in need also exist within the diverse spaces of the city. While there have been a successive number of regeneration projects in the inner-city regions since the 1970s, these display geographically based variations in success. Many of the projects, funded by both government and the private sector, have focused on the Harbour and Quayside and the Eastern areas of the city, where developments of luxury housing, swanky shopping malls and architecturally bold tourist attractions have altered the landscape and brought new opportunities and lifestyles to some. Other districts, such as the south-west of the city have been, as Shirley explains, 'slower to pick up', with a consequent impact on youth employment.

The city council's interventions have focused on increasing the number of apprenticeships, and widening participation and access to these, expanding graduate traineeships, funding a range of employer recruitment incentives to bolster new job opportunities, promoting volunteering as a key plank of both economic and civic policy, and expanding provision of employability training through funding voluntary organizations to run courses. As Shirley succinctly puts it, "there's a whole employability industry out there in Glasgow to support young people towards employment". This includes programmes managed by the Scottish Government and Jobcentre Plus, such as the DWP's Move into Work scheme, which offers work experience (often within the voluntary sector) and employability training to young people aged 18–24 for the first 39 weeks of their unemployment.

Bolstered in part by the Commonwealth Games, the voluntary sector thus plays a central role in the delivery of Glasgow's youth employment strategy, particularly for those aged between 18 and 24 who have 'basically no qualifications, who left school with basically nothing', as Mickey, a trainer and manager at The Volunteer Centre (TVC) outlined to us. A network of voluntary sector organizations, such as TVC, are co-funded by the city council, the Scottish Government and the EU, as well as other charitable organizations such as the Prince's Trust. They receive referrals from Skills Development Scotland, Jobcentre Plus, Jobs in Business Glasgow and agencies working with young people with mental health issues, homelessness and young carers. TVC informed us that it also gets young people turning up 'on spec', having seen their website or marketing, and coming along to see what is on offer. For many, as Michael from the Scottish Government explains, the employability training run by Volunteer Centres "aims at improving job skills ... like turning up on time, numeracy, literacy". However, while a significant number of young people *do* succeed in moving into paid employment or further education, a substantial number do not: nearly 17 per cent become stuck on the roundabouts of the job-seeking ring-road (EY Foundation, 2016). For these, volunteering may not only be, as Michael from the Scottish Government put it, "to a certain extent a stop gap thing" but also a longer-term activity, which takes a long time to, or perhaps never will, lead to paid employment. Our research aimed to find out why.

Case study: Volunteering Makes Sense

When it comes to employability training, 18–24-year-olds can fall into a gap in the market, being neither school leavers nor adults with some history of work behind them. As a consequence, TVC, as manager and trainer Mickey told us on our first research visit to Glasgow, has developed a distinctive project, Volunteering Makes Sense (VMS). VMS is a five-week programme running regularly throughout the year, with each programme recruiting approximately 15 18–24-year-olds from a wide variety of social and educational backgrounds. Participants attend for 16 hours per week, participating in a mixture of classroom-based sessions and 'volunteering tasters', and receiving funding for lunch and travel expenses. In the first week of the programme, each young person samples three different volunteering sites before deciding which they would like to spend more time in for a longer period of work experience. They then continue volunteering for their chosen charity for at least one day a week for the remainder of the course. In addition, participants are helped to identify their transferable workplace skills and develop their CVs, and receive an accredited certificate and references.

To gain a 'hands-on' sense of the experiences of the young people who pass through TVC's doors, we attended two VMS programmes. We learnt that the young people on the course can be a highly diverse group: the first programme we attended, for example, consisted of two international university students looking to use their vacation time profitably to gain skills for future employability, and three partially employed young people working in low-skilled jobs such as fast food outlets but wishing to gain more professional and meaningful work, with the rest (mainly white males) being unemployed with few, or no, educational qualifications, not currently doing much with their time. Some of these were on benefits, and some had learning difficulties, problems at home or mental health issues. Five participants were migrants, from Brunei, Somalia, Libya, Lithuania and South India.

The diversity of participants meant that some were willing and able to be interviewed 'formally', but others were less comfortable with this methodology. However, by attending the programmes every day we slowly developed good relationships with participants, chatting to them informally in class, in the minibus travelling to their work experience placement, and as we volunteered alongside them. Often aided by the content of the programme itself, as well as support from the trainers, our conversations took a lifecourse approach, gradually exploring educational histories, employability and employment experiences, attitudes to volunteering and hopes for the future. We also conducted interviews with trainers at TVC and managers at the organizations where the volunteering took place.

The classroom

Taught components of VMS were conducted in TVC's city-centre headquarters, located on an upper floor of a retail and office block in the heart of Glasgow, with buses from all over the city stopping directly in the street below. The premises are bright and welcoming, open-plan and colourful, with comfy red sofas for sitting and chatting. The main learning space is panoptic: clearly visible behind a glass wall, students can both look out on to the rest of the office as well as be seen by employees and visitors. It is here trainees spend their afternoons, each with their own borrowed laptop, completing a range of online tasks for the Scottish Employability Award, with the support of trainers, Mickey and Tamsin. The mood is open and friendly as the young people josh with their peers, but Mickey and Tamsin keep a close eye, as some can be easily distracted.

On the first day of the programme, Mickey starts the session off with a film about volunteering. We are shown footage of Glasgow, interspersed with interviews and shots of volunteering in action: environmental conservation, golf coaching, percussion workshops, teaching English to asylum seekers and helping out at Mary's Meals, a charity that aims to provide hungry children with a daily school meal. Neoliberal policy rhetoric echoes through the voiceover, as we are told that volunteering:

> gives us huge benefits: confidence, work experience, secure employment, lots of fun, a real buzz ... a chance to be to be part of something bigger.

As we then settle down to work, it is clear that Mickey and Tamsin's approach combines a high degree of sensitivity to the young people's individual positions with an awareness of government expectations of the learning outcomes of the training. Both have worked with young people for many years, and they know that programmes such as VMS tend to cater for those who fall outside of the 'blue-chip' employability schemes offered within the city. Typically, their programmes cater for young people with 'accelerated transition' experiences (Wade and Dixon, 2006: 200), such as leaving the parental home early, coming out of care or becoming parents in their teens. Some have mental health or other disability issues, caring responsibilities or custodial sentences, and many failed at school: "I was one of the lowest there", Oliver, one of the course participants, tells us. The consequence is often an extended period of liminality, being neither in education nor work. In the classroom, a key challenge is tackling the low levels of self-confidence possessed by many of the young people. We see that they struggle to connect their own experiences with the discourses and language of the online workbooks they are supposed to be completing and, as Mickey puts it, "identify skills that you already possess and how you can transfer these to the workplace". Mickey and Tamsin encourage the young people to try to reconceptualize their everyday experiences within the language of employability:

> 'Think about things you've done in the past and things you learned and gained from that – could be anything, some of you may think you have not really done anything, and

not got any skills, but *everyone* has skills, even if you have never had a job – if you have been in a club, played sport, volunteered, you'll have picked up skills, even looking after you little brother, you will have picked things up. We're going to help you identify these skills and how they can help you into employment. We're going to do a mind map – anyone know what a mind map is?'

Mickey demonstrates on the flipchart board at the front of the room:

'You start with a blank sheet, start with yourself in the middle. Put up things you've done and what skills you have gained for doing that: volunteering = teamwork, gardening. Playing football = communication, teamwork. Run own household? = budgeting, organisational skills. Do this for yourselves, one for the present and one for the past. This is the first piece of evidence for your qualifications.'

The task demands that the young people reframe their identities within a new language. Some, such as Matthew, White and in his mid-twenties, who was referred to TVC through yet another work programme provider, found this difficult, as our fieldnotes demonstrate:

'I don't do nothing' Matthew says. Mickey tries to help him: do you walk the dogs or help out in the house? Do the washing up or look after any of your family, a little brother, your gran? Matthew walks his grandpa's dogs every night, so Mickey tells him, 'well, there you are, you have to organize your time to fit that in every night', but Matthew isn't convinced, 'I just do it whenever I'm there, so they can go to the toilet'. Mickey persists, but Matthew is adamant he doesn't do anything – or at least, 'nothing that I can put down on here!' Mickey asks him what he does do all day then? He plays PlayStation – FIFA – with his friends. 'Well, you must have to communicate and work as a team on some of those games then, do you organize that?' 'No', Matthew replies, 'I just go on and see who's there. But I am in a flute band'. A flute band is a part of the sectarian Orange Walks, to celebrate the defeat of Catholicism and the victory of the Prince of Orange. They are very controversial. Matthew left school at 16 and wishes he could go back and do it all again to get better results, as he went to his exams stoned. He only did well in maths, where he got a 3, the only result he is proud of. Matthew and Oliver dutifully write down the skills that Tamsin and Mickey suggest to them from the activities they do – but say that they haven't heard of some of the words before. Then we learn that Matthew has done some labouring for his Dad's company, joinery, fitting kitchens. He asks, 'is "dependable" a word?'

We also work away at the tasks, which we too find challenging. We are asked 'What are you good at? How will this help you in the world of work?'. We notice that some of the young people sit staring at their laptops, not writing anything, such as Martin, who is only 18, but seems older, quite withdrawn and sad: 'like the stuffing has been knocked out of him' Mickey notes after the session is finished.

The next day, we are joined in the classroom by another trainer, Douglas. Matthew is still struggling: 'This is why I don't apply for jobs. It is a hassle!'. Douglas agrees, 'it is a hassle, it's not exciting or interesting, but you have to do it if you want a job. This is what you are here for – to take away the confusion and help you'. Douglas works with Matthew – 'when an employer's looks at the application form, they want to know you've looked at the advert, and can do the work: if you've worked in a kitchen, laboured stacking wood, skills you can transfer to another setting. Just have a stab, it's just an exercise'. Matthew seems to be getting anxious about the task, so Douglas hopes to calm him down.

He goes to help Andrew, reading what he has done and declares it a good first draft. 'I think there's more that you can say though, I'd give it a 5/10 if I saw that as an employer. It's a good opening: "I think I'd be good at this job because of my past experience" – now add in where you were and what you did. You've introduced it well, now just explain what you did – be detailed, say that you used different mop heads or cleaned different surfaces, or the types of cleaning products that you used. Make them think "this guy is worth an interview!". Fill the page. Put that you are a hard worker, not that you were. Have another stab. Anyone else need a hand?'

Douglas jokes that he hates applications forms, but it's a large empty box that you can use to really impress: 'It is a large empty box, but you need to stop thinking about it as an empty box. If you carry on volunteering, you will have stuff to write in that box'.

Enabling young people to have the confidence and material to fill 'the empty box' in meaningful ways is one of the key challenges facing employability organizations such as TVC. Trainers are tasked with 'a conduct of conduct' application of power, that aims to 'regenerate' the young person by 'endeavour[ing] to shape, guide, direct the conduct of others … it embraces the ways in which one might be urged and enacted to bridle one's own passions, to control one's own instincts, to govern oneself' (Rose, 1989: 3). To achieve this, trainers need to teach the young people a new language by which to position themselves: a language that may feel foreign and bear no relation to how they understand themselves and their own experiences. The discourse of responsible employability demands that young people conform to expectations of individualization, responsibilization and 'work readiness'. Those participants attending higher education were able to get on and complete the tasks individually and without difficulty, but most of the trainees lacked adequate cultural capital and personal resources to do so, and needed constant support and guidance. The trainers' response was to broker the employability discourse with pragmatism, working hard to improve the young people's senses of self-worth where they could. At the same time, encouraging self-governance in the young people was evidenced in the way they steered the young people not only to use the language of employability to reframe themselves 'on paper' but, in the process, to bring multiple meanings to the notion of 'responsibilization' to recognize the very real circumstances and contexts embedded within them. At the same time, trainers retained a realistic awareness that the challenges that many of the young people face in their lives may mean that, for some of them, 'work readiness' is a distant goal. As we now turn to show, such sensitivity was differentially shared by those managing the work experience elements of the programme.

Volunteer tasters

The trainees' work experience sessions are spent in very different landscapes to TVC's city-centre premises. Most of the work experience is conducted south of the River Clyde, in districts where the architecture still kindles memories of Glasgow's economic past. Govan, once home to the heavy industries of iron and steel, engineering and shipbuilding, provided Glaswegians with employment opportunities from the mid-1800s to the 1950s (Gomez, 1998). The Gorbals was where the industrial workers lived, heavily overcrowded and associated with high levels of poverty and crime (Smith, 2014). The decline of manufacturing meant that, by the middle of the 20th century, these districts had become economically and physically depleted. Today, the economic and social challenges associated with unemployment, poverty and population mobility still present themselves, and youth unemployment, vulnerable people and alcohol remain over-represented in the Greater Govan area (GCPP, 2013). To tackle this, the city has made the special architectural character of the area the focus of a townscape heritage initiative, and voluntary organizations are springing up in many of the change-of-use buildings, aiming to build on strong senses of place attachment to improve local social capital building (Putnam, 2000). Old warehouses and chapels, once abandoned, are slowly being converted into community cafés, playcentres and creative arts hubs, and long-neglected tenement squares are being transformed into recreation parks and community gardens. Mirroring the transitions of the young people on the training, the neighbourhood is undergoing a process of 'regeneration', refashioned and enhanced. Sam, who manages a community gardening project, provides us with more information for our fieldnotes:

Tenement Gardens (TG) is based in public gardens in the Gorbals, in the heart of the old high-rise tenement blocks. Until a few years ago, the gardens had gone to 'wrack and ruin, totally overrun by weeds and mostly used as a drinking den'. Now the area is undergoing redevelopment with a mixture of social and market housing; some of the older tenements refurbished to a high level of specification. An attractive public greenscape is part of this gentrification process, but TG also aim to encourage healthy eating and food recycling amongst the local community. They grow fruit and vegetables to give away in return for deposits of food waste. Everything is grown from scratch – carrots, onions, beans, herbs: all organic and fresh, relying on volunteers, including a regular supply of young people from TVC, to do all the groundwork. Mickey jokes: 'Not a great one to do if it's raining as it's outside!'.

These liminal landscapes, newly positioned as they are betwixt their former, neglected state and the more heavily resourced and modernized areas of the city centre, suggest new possibilities. These are reflected in the sorts of volunteering activities conducted by the small but often resourceful voluntary organizations that are working to regenerate the area: whether by reimagining a once-abandoned space for local artwork, coffee and companionship, recycling clothes and furniture for affordable consumption, or refiguring the streetscape with free-to-pick vegetable planters, their aim is to support community change. For this reason, many are keen to become involved in the city's youth employment initiatives and support local young people in their own transitions. The Studio, for example, a café run as a social enterprise by Andy, is based in an old industrial unit now used for exhibitions, workshops, craft fairs and artists' studios. Not far away is Secondtimearound, an unwanted goods depository that aims to recycle furniture, light goods and kitchenware, selling at little or no cost to low-income families. Around the corner is the charity shop, Marketplace. Together with TG, these organizations receive a regular supply of young people from TVC for work experience. However, their approach to the young people's training varies considerably. As managers negotiate their positions with, and 'disciplinary' power relations towards, the trainees, subtle mechanisms of power–knowledge and surveillance worked to shape the participants' self-understandings and activities in diverse ways (Hodge and Harris, 2012).

At one end of the spectrum, managers such as Andy at The Studio attempt to give young people opportunities to develop skills through meaningful training. As such, surveillance was focused on individual needs and developing capabilities, as our fieldnotes reveal:

Initially the young people are very shy, not wanting to choose between the options of kitchen work, coffee-making or waitering. Andy is very kind, offering them all coffee and having a chat before they decide. Then Paul who runs the kitchen intercedes and demands 'help now!'. As they are standing closest, Oliver and Pina are given aprons and get stuck in making coleslaw.

Andy is interested in the young volunteers, asking them what they want to do, if they have done this before. He spends time with them, showing them how to do things: make a coffee, polish and roll the cutlery. Paul is the same in the kitchen. Oliver reveals he wants to go into the Marines, and Paul was in the army too, so tells him a few stories. Andy says that they have a lot of volunteers come through, and they usually end up getting jobs after a week or two so while that is great for them, it would be nice to have some stay on a bit longer. They have gone on to different jobs: a bank, Costa coffee and all sorts, mostly due to raised confidence, Andy thinks. He and Paul get the young people talking more than we have ever seen before: Andy treats them as adults and talks to them on the level. The young people like the chilled-out atmosphere here. Paul himself started as a volunteer, then Jobs and Businesses Glasgow paid half his salary to begin with.

After all the cutlery is polished and rolled, Paul ushers us into the kitchen to bake a carrot cake. Pina is really keen on this and follows, finding where the aprons are. Following a recipe, Paul divvies up the jobs, claiming that he is no baker himself. Andy and Paul are both generous, giving out coffees so the young people can practise making them, giving us slices of cake and engaging the young people in conversation about the Scottish referendum. All the young people like the café, Paul and Andy.

Oliver tells us how pleased he is that Andy has invited him back the next day. He tells us he learnt how to make coffee, then while he was making his very first one, Andy took a phone call. The next thing Oliver knew, ten customers had arrived and so he had to take all their orders and start making coffees double quick! Baptism of fire nonetheless! Oliver says that he's been told in these situations you have to take the initiative and get on with it. When he noticed that someone was finished with a plate he went to ask for it.

The following week, Oliver and Isabella tell Tamsin they are going to be put through a first aid course by Andy at the cafe. Pina also wants to go. This will be a valuable skill for all of them.

Andy and Paul are committed to enhancing the skill sets of young people, and while they are, as Eri tells us, "nice, supportive, teaching me how to do it", they also demonstrate real trust in the young people's capabilities by throwing them in at the deep end, leaving them to sink or swim, cope with customers, and make coleslaw, cakes and coffee. In the opportunity these experiences offer the young people to 'recombine new and existing cultural resources and experience new ways of relating' (Howard-Grenville et al, 2011: 523), we could see how they grew in confidence. Isabella, a young migrant from Lithuania, smiled when we asked about her morning, proclaiming, "I've got new skills!".

While Andy and Paul's starting point is the young people themselves, their approach is also a further example of the operationalization of Foucauldian concepts of the self. As they work alongside the young people, giving them support, taking time to talk to each of them and allocating tasks to build confidence as well as technical skills, they are simultaneously supporting the young people to develop a specific version of the self, one that is fit for outward approval by customers and conforms to expectations of good service. The young people come to learn which performances are externally validated and rewarded as likely to lead to paid employment.

Sam at TG also aimed to give the young people meaningful training that would meet external expectations. However, young people are, of course, highly diverse in terms of interests and ambitions, and gardening is not for everyone. Indeed, it is a challenge for TVC to find placements that are both constructive in developing skills and also appeal to the individual young people who attend the programmes. While some may find satisfaction in one occupational sector, others may be less inspired, as our fieldnotes reveal:

Sam takes the young people around the beds, explaining crops and getting them to harvest the ripe runner beans. Slowly, they get stuck in. Martin and Isabella aren't really too keen on the idea at first. Isabella tells me she used to do a lot of vegetable-growing in her village in Lithuania, and it was always a chore. Martin admits he is not a big fruit and veg man. Amir seems keen though, given that he only eats raw food; he takes photos of the plants and seems interested in the variety of vegetables. Martin hangs back but eventually helps, Isabella does what she is asked, but doesn't seem wholly impressed by the work. Mickey the trainer from TVC is also with us, cheerfully encouraging the young people in their tasks, making jokes and asking questions about the gardens. Sam walks us round several different sites, shows us how to harvest and implant with new crops in the small corners that become empty. He demonstrates how to prick out seedlings and where to plant them. He encourages us to taste and smell the plants and remove dead leaves for compost. There is some heavy lifting for those that want something more physical, and lighter work for others. His enthusiasm is infectious to some, but not all: Amir is really keen and wants to return, he really likes the Gardens and although not related to the kind of work he hopes to go into – computing – he enjoys it. He is glad to be volunteering as usually he would just stay in bed sleeping late: it's good to be up and doing something instead, he says.

Foucault's governmentality approach, which focuses on 'the point at which things are taking place' (Foucault, 2007: 46), is valuable to explore how practices differ in different contexts at the micro-level. At The Studio and TG, while the approach was to micro-manage the conduct of the self – the ways in which the young people present themselves and operate in the world – there was also an aim to empower young people with useful skills and, by raising their self-confidence, encourage them to position themselves with more agency. This was not universal across the young people's volunteering experiences, however, as our fieldnotes recording our first morning at Marketplace show:

> The shop's manager, Ivana, allocates us tasks. She asks if anyone has used tills before and several have. She has Hama work near the tills as she has experience, but she asks her to come to her if anyone wants to pay for anything. We are soon all busy cleaning and dusting shelves and crockery, sorting shoes and handbags, making sure the best ones are the most obvious in the middle shelves, moving any to recycling if they are dirty or broken and unlikely to sell.

> Everyone is shy and quiet at the start, none volunteer for the different jobs, but slowly get started and gradually begin to talk to each other. When they finish one job they go on to something else, sorting, cleaning and tidying the shop. We are there for a couple of hours: we are getting thirsty and a bit grubby and no one has mentioned where the toilet is. Ivana has disappeared, so we work

unsupervised. Hama tells us she hated the morning, as she was just cleaning glass cabinets which she disliked a lot.

Forbidden to engage directly with customers or work on the tills, the young people are marginalized to the back spaces, cleaning and sorting 'rubbish' (Gregson and Crewe, 2003). Time passes slowly; the work does not inspire them. It is not what they imagined doing, and this is made worse by the fact that they are only given perfunctory 'training', relegated to low-level tasks and then left unsupervised. For the work experience placements to be of real value for the young people, TVC must rely on the professionalism of local managers to provide training and support; but some, like Ivana, saw the young people's time as something just to be filled. For others, it was something to be wasted, as is clear from our fieldnotes:

Andrew went to his placement at Secondtimearound yesterday but it didn't go well. He was hoping to be moving furniture and doing heavy-lifting but instead was left in a room on his own all morning and told to clean a fridge (with a toothbrush). He says it was 'a rubbish experience'. Later that afternoon Micky tells me about the conversation he had with Secondtimearound. They called him to say they didn't want Andrew back, but were vague why. Micky pushed them, and they said that he hadn't completed the task he was given. Micky argued on Andrew's behalf – it was his first day, you couldn't expect him to get everything right straight away. He was shocked at their attitude. He asked for more feedback, and they said he made a mess, didn't clear up after himself and those who worked with Andrew weren't happy to see him again. Andrew suffers from schizophrenia and could really do with some support and encouragement. 'He's a volunteer' says Micky, 'you have to support people when they volunteer with you, not expect them to know everything straight away, that's the point, they're there to learn'. Micky was really disappointed with the attitude of the manager, particularly as 'they are a charity, it's not on for a charity not to be supportive of someone like Andrew. He's 26 and it's not his first job but he still needs to be given a chance, helped to get on'.

Micky decides they will not use this organisation again. When Andrew asks about going back there, Micky cuts him off and says 'We're not sending you back there – you're a volunteer, even if you did make a mess, and I bet you didn't, they should have said that to you while you were there and asked you to clean it up. They say you didn't complete tasks, well, they should have been there to tell you to finish one thing before moving on to the next one. Volunteers need help and support and showing what to do – it's not rocket science. Not happy with their attitude which is why we're not sending Pina there'.

Analysis of the young people's work placement experiences thus reveals real divergence in approach by employers and managers towards the employability of young people. On the one hand, managers of local community projects such as those at The Studio and TG recognized the value that good-quality training can offer in terms of young people's engagement and sense of purpose as well as raising confidence, skills levels and, potentially, chances of paid employment. They fully acknowledged that the young people were volunteering in order to learn workplace skills and, as such, saw it as their *responsibility* to be proactive in developing their training in meaningful ways. However, at the same time, this involved them in shaping and validating a very particular set of subjectivities and performances, which conformed to market expectations of 'good service' within the hospitality sector.

In marked contrast, however, other managers, such as those at Marketplace and Secondtimearound, positioned the young people's employability training as the responsibility of others. *Absolving* themselves of the need to offer good-quality training, they occupied the young people with unsupervised, time-filling exercises, with little opportunity for self-development. Adopting this position risks that young people, especially those with diverse needs, are set up to fail to meet the objectives of the training programmes.

Discussion

Our interviews with local policy makers in Glasgow demonstrated that, while they aligned themselves quite closely with national policies, these were then spatialized and differentialized according to the specific challenges of Glasgow's distinctive history and its impact on youth employment (Shaw and MacKinnon, 2011; Woolvin et al, 2015). To use Alcock's (2012) terminology, Scotland's, and more specifically, Glasgow's, 'governance space' appears visible in the delivery of youth employment policy. Scotland is perceived by many as a 'happening place' (Mooney and Poole, 2004: 459) in relation to social policy innovation, and this indeed appeared to be a motivation for many of the policy makers we spoke to, who were keen to build on regional opportunities such as the Commonwealth Games to develop a dynamic, local response to employment challenges. Recognizing that many of Glasgow's traditional entry routes into work have disappeared, particularly for those with no or few formal educational qualifications, but that slowly emerging in their stead is a range of diverse enterprises and local initiatives aiming to revitalize communities and opportunities, local voluntary organizations are selected and funded to run bespoke employability programmes embedded in the city's distinctive geography. Yet while their aim is to increase overall levels of youth employment, policy makers acknowledge that different young people and different city regions have diverse needs and, therefore, a range of outcomes will qualify as 'success'. As one key informant interviewee put it, "we are equally happy if they [young people facing specific challenges] are taking steps towards employment".

Our ethnography and interviews with TVC informed us how trainers too recognized the diversity in individual capabilities and needs and tailored their approach towards employability outcomes accordingly. Their primary aim was to support the young people who came through their doors in appropriate ways, primarily through raising levels of self-confidence. The diversity of programme participants puts flesh on the bones of the abstract subjects of national policy discourses: ungendered, classed and raced, devoid of specific biographies, needs and responsibilities. While trainers worked hard, and in many ways skilfully, to teach the 'language' of employability – both oral and embodied – they also recognized that this was not the most suitable outcome for all the participants on their programmes. More realistic was the aim of enhancing levels of self-worth, through participation in local communities, which were themselves undergoing processes of regeneration to transform spatial understandings and identities. Thus, for trainers, the more traditional discourse of volunteering as active citizenship was intertwined with that of responsible employability in their approach to governing young people through 'employability training'.

However, it must also be acknowledged that this position is reinforced by the lack of engagement with, and by, businesses within the private sector with the young people's training. Restricting work experience placements to the voluntary sector alone, whether by choice or necessity, means that the young people's experience may not always be accepted as transferable and valuable by employers in other contexts. While the relationship between goods and value is unclear and complex (Gregson and Crewe, 2003), a charity shop in the Gorbals reselling unwanted cast-offs, for example, is on the margins of dominant cultural meanings of retail, fashion and consumption, more typically found in Glasgow's main upmarket shopping area Style Mile. Spatial, cultural and economic liminality can position the young people on the borders of the sites where higher value is attached. Further, the lack of paid work opportunities within the voluntary sector may mean that some of the young people are being potentially locked into long-term unemployment and risks of social exclusion. While volunteering, for these young people, is a 'step towards employability', the road for many is, as yet, still long.

SIX

Conclusion: Inequality, Liminality and Risk

Introduction

The chapters of this book have built up a picture of youth employability training in the UK as framed by powerful national policy discourses, translated through regional policy strategies into a variety of entry route schemes, operationalized in practice by trainers, local employers providing work experience, and experienced by young people from wide-ranging and diverse social and educational backgrounds. Building our picture of youth employability training has required drawing together critical and historical analyses of national and regional youth employment and training policies, and the debates and controversies around these, with our on-the-ground ethnographic research. Plaiting these together, we have explored the complex landscapes of youth employability training to fulfil three aims: to investigate what it is like for young people to undergo employability training as a pathway into work in the current context in the UK; to capture the voices, strategies and motivations of local policy makers, training providers and young people; and to contribute theoretically to understanding of youth employability policy and training. In terms of the latter, we have adopted the theoretical lens of a post-Foucauldian governmentality approach, which has proved valuable in informing the way in which we have approached and analyzed the 'discursive field:' the national and regional policy spaces where the 'problems' of youth employability and training are identified and solutions proposed, as well as the 'interventionist practices', as demonstrated in the four training programmes investigated through our empirical research.

What the post-Foucauldian emphasis on the power–knowledge relationship between the contemporary, dominant framing of policy on young people, un/employment and skills, and the ensuing technologies of youth governance foregrounds most dramatically is the pervasive force of neoliberalism. This operates as an overarching, structuring discourse that articulates through the ways that young people's transitions into and within the labour market are constructed and experienced. Resonating throughout our analyses are the ways in which the free-market logic seeps into every encounter by young people with education, training and work, structuring both the 'getting in' and the 'getting on'. In this way, as Ong (2006: 3) explains:

> Neoliberalism can also be conceptualized as a new relationship between government and knowledge through which governing activities are recast as nonpolitical and non-ideological problems that need technical solutions. Indeed, neoliberalism considered as a technology of government is a profoundly active way of rationalising governing and self-governing in order to 'optimise'. The spread of neoliberal calculation as a governing technology is thus a historical process that unevenly articulates situated political constellations.

Our research has demonstrated how neoliberal conceptual beliefs and practices, such as individualization, responsibilization, flexibility and participation, are thoroughly implicated in youth employment policy and training practice. These not only shape the structures of inequality and power that impact on the opportunities and constraints facing different groups of young people in the UK, but resonate through, and are reproduced by, the everyday assumptions of policy makers, the curriculum design of training programmes, the approaches and responses of employers and the subjectivities, understandings and decisions of young people themselves. This is well exemplified by the employability training in the North East. While this brought clear and positive effects for young trainees, it also required subjugation to an externally validated set of skills and behaviours perceived to be desirable by employers. That the programme had been designed by young people themselves reveals the power of the technologies of governance in the shaping of subjectivities. At the other end of the class spectrum, the interns at Global Accountants, while highly rewarded, also learned that they had to construct subjectivities within a narrow range of prescribed neoliberal performances in order to get in and get on.

The research also makes obvious how the constraints faced by, and opportunities permitted to, young people are shaped by the broad and complex interplay of historical events, economic processes such as globalization, industrial and manufacturing decline, the spread of a free-market logic, and cycles of economic volatility, as well as social and cultural constructions of young people through employment-related policy responses and local communities. These are all further fragmented geographically, such that they play out and are performed with diversity across the different economic regions of the UK. Place clearly matters, with young people in Scotland and the North East positioned within labour markets needing to redefine themselves with new opportunities after successive and substantial periods of industrial decline, while those on the South Coast, located within striking distance of London and the South East, both prioritized in the UK's economy, face a more buoyant labour market. Those in London are able to enjoy the benefits of the capital's position in the global economy and its ability to weather economic volatility, although, as we write, the effects of the UK's intended withdrawal from the EU have yet to be fully determined.

But the picture is far from a deterministic one. For we also signal the processes by which young people, and, more often than not, their trainers, negotiate and enact these subjectivities, highlighting that in practice, dominant discourses and subject positions can be challenged, modified and reframed. Our case study in Glasgow, for example, revealed the ways in which trainers actively disrupt messages from employers that they regard as unacceptable, recognizing that young people have highly diverse needs and capabilities. Many of the young people we talked to, whether deciding accountancy was not for them, or trying to access the music industry in the North East, were clear that they were holding out for a career that they felt passionate about, rather than just taking 'any job'. The picture is, therefore, far more complex than merely one of 'young people as victims' of historical, economic, political and social processes. As our theoretical position makes clear, we understand young people as, to an extent, free agents, able to make (some) choices as to what sort of work they do or do not want to do, and how they want to live their lives more generally. In interplay with the intersecting strategies of trainers and work experience providers, young people from diverse social and regional backgrounds may be harnessed with the confidence, resources, resilience and dispositions either to access work and careers of choice or make other lifestyle decisions. Nevertheless, these 'choices' are shaped by social structures and dominant discourses that often function only to reproduce, or further entrench, social inequalities, positions of liminality, and vulnerability to risk across the different regional economies of the UK. These four themes – regionality, social inequality, liminality and risk – repeatedly emerge through the chapters of this book as of key significance for understanding youth employability in the UK. As such, in this final chapter, while it is important to recognize that these themes interplay, we explore each in turn.

Regionality and youth employability

As is now well established, the organization of labour is thoroughly shaped by space and place, with distinctive and shifting geographical outcomes (Halford et al, 2015). Massey's account of place (1994) articulates how place is a dynamic '... node in network of relations' (Glucksmann, 2000: 131), both local and global, that combine to produce distinctive combinations of culture, community and identity: a sense of 'what it's like around here' (Glucksmann, 2000: 146). This rich understanding integrates the subjective meanings of lived place, with an appreciation of other, multiple and diverse relations, such as historical economic shifts, national and regional government policies, global and national finance, regeneration strategies and community activism. Combined, these are all just part of an immense range of influences that contribute to the making of place. Place thus comes to be understood as a point of intersection, produced from the interactions of relations 'from the immensity of the global to the intimately tiny' (Massey, 2005: 9).

This approach is a helpful tool to apply to the UK's youth labour market. It is well known that this displays distinctive geographies, linked both to spatial divisions of labour and sectoral cultures, many of which increasingly pull economic activity towards the UK's South East. However, we have less detailed knowledge of how training programmes interact with this geography, and the role they play within 'the overall articulation of interconnected work activities' (Glucksmann, 2005: 21) as they are constituted in particular times and places. The case study approach within this book contributes to our understanding of these processes, by showing how youth labour markets are made 'on the ground', in the life stories and everyday practices of the young people, the trainers who work to support them and the employers who provide them with work experience that may or may not lead to offers of employment. In doing so, and this is critical to our argument, we also demonstrate how the everyday activities and experiences of youth employability training are not only a local matter, but rather are the effects of the stretching of economic, political and social relations over space and time, constructed at the interlocking scales of individuals, communities, regions and nations (Dyck, 2005; Halford et al, 2015).

Our chapters thus not only reveal how youth labour markets are made in place and the role training providers play in this, but also the significance of place to shaping the identities and prospects of local young people. As we discussed in Chapter Two, while many of the young people in our research demonstrated a strong attachment to place, many were also *stuck* in place, lacking the resources to travel any more than walking distance or a bus ride to work. Where a young person lives is critical to the range of options in front of them. In Glasgow, for example, the particular history of the city's unemployment, the hosting of the Commonwealth Games, and the ongoing regeneration processes to tackle urban decline through transforming local spaces, all feed into a culture of voluntarism. Not only does this sector offer employment (either paid or unpaid) to the adult labour market, but it is also the voluntary sector that, in turn, plays a key role in supporting local young people in their skills training and development. What this means, however, is that *unpaid* work is often both a means and an outcome of the training programme, thus further contributing to the significance of voluntarism within the wider regional workforce.

In the North East, the history of industrial decline is in many ways similar to Glasgow's, but here specific industrial sectors are targeted and supported by government as a means to regenerate the local economy. These are largely 'new industries', such as digital technologies, which rely on highly skilled employees. As yet, however, these are not actively connecting with the skills development of local young people, meaning they do not offer a viable pipeline to employment opportunities. In spite of the fact that the prioritizing of high-skilled, high-tech employers means that the youth labour remains depressed, and, as such, many of the young people see little hope of getting into regular, secure, well-paid employment in the region. Many we talked to revealed strong attachments to place, telling us how they felt they 'belonged' in the area and did not want to leave. This was 'home'.

In some contrast to both Glasgow and the North East, the South Coast's history of small businesses is held up to foster a spirit of enterprise. This is used to frame training opportunities and support for young people, in turn enhancing this as a distinctive feature of the region. The notion of a young person being their own employer as a solution to un/employment was not something we encountered elsewhere through our discussions with policy makers, trainers and young people. However, the young people's futures were uncertain, the success of their businesses unproven and subject to a myriad of complex economic, political and cultural factors. This in turn feeds into the instability of the local youth labour market.

In contrast again were the opportunities available in London, where big business clusters. Here the scale and capacity of both training and employment opportunities mean that young people are not only more able to 'get in' but also 'get on'. It was often this sense of opportunity, as well as the 'buzz' of London as a global city, that attracted young (and, admittedly, more highly skilled) young people to want to work and live there. However, as we turn to discuss in the next section, opportunities are not evenly available to all young people, with social background playing a discriminating role.

It is clear from our case studies that local youth labour markets are profoundly shaped by relations to place, and that these relations are heterogenous, produced at the intersection of multiple relations and processes. This is emphatically *not* to say, however, that each of our case studies is 'representative' of all youth employability training within each place: not only will there be differences with other programmes in the region offering the same form of employability training, but each region also offers a full range of different training programmes to young people, through which more differences undoubtedly exist. Theoretically, however, we would expect there to be some enduring and stable connections, as places are not infinitely plastic (Halford et al, 2105). Further, and importantly, it was often the attachments between people and place that produced an unwillingness of young people to leave their local area and the dedication of trainers to support them in their quest to stay. For many, remaining in the place in which they felt comfortable was more important than securing paid employment. It is crucial that policy makers and employers understand this.

The endurance of social inequality

One of the strongest themes uniting the chapters in the book is that social class inequalities 'remain in enduring and familiar ways in the lives of young people' (France and Roberts, 2017: 135). Our investigation of each of our four training schemes reveals how, even in times of the expansion of higher education, changing demographic employment scripts and improvements in gender equality, class remains fundamental for young people in terms of access to good-quality training and aspirations for future careers. In our study of employability training in the North East, we saw how the discourse of employability is on the one hand reinforced by the course at YVNE, as it sought to develop particular skills and traits in the participants. However, efforts to subvert this focused on moving away from seeing young people as in deficit and orientating their training to helping them realize what they already know about employment and find ways to articulate and evidence this to employers. Despite this, the influence of social class was evident, as most of the young people who participated did lack a range of capitals, both in terms of family resources and wider networks to access social and cultural capital, that could lead to work. In particular, both aspiration and opportunities were depressed in Hartlepool, in common with other rural and coastal communities (Spielhofer et al, 2011; Donnelly and Evans, 2016). Although the region had a proactive LEP aware of growth sectors, both this information and support for routes into these fields was not available for those working with YVNE, whose networks were limited in the opportunities they could offer to participants.

In our discussion of enterprise initiatives on the South Coast, we saw how enterprise is adopted as a key plank for employability at SEU, a non-elite university, renowned for its widening participation approach, diverse student intake and flexibility in terms of Level 3 entry grades. Students at SEU are most likely to be state educated and the first generation to participate in higher education. Our discussions with trainers and programme leaders informed us how this group of young people were seen from the start as facing challenges with future employment, despite the fact that the South has recovered comparatively more strongly from the decline in the traditional manufacturing industries and cyclical recessions (Martin et al, 2016) than other regions such as the North East. This is in part due to less dependence on the public sector for employment than, for example, the North East, and the more diversified 'industrial portfolio' (Conroy, 1975) that tends to exist in the region. A history of small businesses and enterprises means that this type of employment is also seen as a viable route for young people who are supported and funded accordingly, through programmes such as those at SEU and EY. While at EY the social backgrounds of the young people were more diverse, most participants lacked substantial financial support from family, had tried, and failed, to secure good-quality employment in other fields, and posited that it was 'down to them' to actively negotiate their future employment trajectories – often the preserve of young people from lower socioeconomic backgrounds (Brooks and Everett, 2009; Borlagdan, 2015). Social class, as well as gender, was further demonstrated in the variations in confidence levels between EY participants about the success of their ventures, as well as in how modest or ambitious their business plans were (Roberts and Evans, 2013, Wilde and Leonard, 2018). Further, as discussed earlier, this form of employment is far from secure, and thus class not only shapes the getting in to this form of employment, but may be remade through its uncertainty.

The research on internships revealed starkly how family background plays a powerful determining role in terms of who gets 'good' and 'poor' workplace training and work experience, and ease of transitions into employment. It is well established that young people have very uneven experiences in terms of distribution of unemployment, underemployment and job precariousness (Felstead et al, 2018), and our case study reminded us how differences *between* graduates, as well as graduates and non-graduates, are a significant point of comparison (France and Roberts, 2017). We saw how middle-class young people attending elite (middle-class) universities were more likely to access increased levels of both family *and* organizational support. Their ability to get in to blue-chip internship programmes (see also Shade and Jacobson, 2015 for a similar finding in Canada), which then resulted in 'getting on' in terms of swift offers of well-paid employment, contrasted bluntly with the experiences of other young people on less prestigious internship schemes. While the latter group also, in the main, had higher education qualifications, that these were obtained at 'local', non-Russell Group (working-class) universities mattered: as often as not, their qualifications did not provide enough cultural and social capital to get them into good-quality training and work. This entry route scheme provided an important reminder of how institutions – educational, family and corporate – consolidate class advantage.

Our interviews with trainers and young people on the volunteering programme in Scotland underscored how low attainment at school has strong connections with being working class (Tomlinson, 2013). Those with negative school experiences and poor educational qualifications were heavily over-represented on the programme, with many having left school only to cycle through a succession of employability programmes of one sort or another. Many also faced other disadvantages, similarly associated with vulnerability to exclusion, such as housing challenges, lack of family support, lone parenthood and/or health issues. At the same time, many within this group, in common with their peers in the North East, revealed strong attachments to place, and found the idea of leaving the area both challenging and risky. The volunteering programme's reliance on local charities to provide (low-skilled) workplace experience, and the lack of engagement of city businesses to provide anything in the way of upskilling, compounded class disadvantage. For the young people on this programme, 'Upward social mobility, especially for those at the "bottom of the pile" remains highly improbable' (France and Roberts, 2017: 83).

In terms of the resolute traction of social class on young people's employment opportunities, the findings from our research are certainly not new. However, this is not to say they are unimportant, for the fact that, in spite of all the energy and funding put into youth employability training, social class prevails as a key determinant of material outcomes provides yet more substance to the call that youth employment policy needs a complete overhaul. The pivotal point is that processes at the macro level – deindustrialization, flexibilization of the labour market, narrowing regional economies, the hollowing out of state responsibility for young people's career's advice, rising tuition fees, to name but a few – are fundamentally shaping opportunities, or lack of opportunities, at the local level. Shifting the lens away from a myopic focus on the individual young person to fully embrace and work with regional economic factors is critical.

Liminal landscapes of youth employability

While understanding youth as 'a liminal stage' is somewhat of an orthodoxy in social science literature (Turner, 1974;

Blatterer, 2010a; Brown et al, 2012), we argue that by adding nuance to the concept we can increase our understanding of the landscapes of youth employability. Building on our previous discussion of regionality, we suggest that the concept is helpful in looking at youth in terms of temporality as well as the way in which young people are emplaced. Turner (1974) drew on Van Gennep's (1960) notion of temporal liminality to describe the in-between phase of young people's 'rites of passage' trajectories, where 'separation' from one stage has been achieved, but not, as yet, 'aggregation' to the next. Turner (1974: 232) conceptualized youth as a 'state of "incompleteness"; neither "child nor adult", "here nor there"' (Blatterer, 2010a: 69). While recent contributors contest any simplistic equating of transitional experiences and (biological) adolescence, arguing that neoliberal contexts and post-industrial labour market conditions have increasingly led to multiple, non-uniform and complex transitions across the whole of the lifecourse (Helve and Evans, 2013), research continues to demonstrate that a period of liminal 'becoming' features in the post-childhood phase of many young people before independent lifestyles and responsibilities are fully acquired (France and Roberts, 2015: 215).

Liminality is not only temporal but has *spatial* qualities. Simmel (1994) conceptualized the liminal as a threshold – a transitional landscape of both physical and psychic possibility (Andrews and Roberts, 2012). Regenerating urban landscapes can also therefore be understood as intrinsically liminal (Crouch, 2012), the concept offering the granularity to heighten understandings of certain places as 'betwixt and between' (Turner, 1974), spatially, temporally and psychically in a state of transformation and becoming. Extending further, we suggest that many of the organizations involved in the governance of youth employability can *also* be conceptualized as betwixt and between: these were often liminal *physically*, in terms of their urban emplacement, *culturally*, in terms of their distance from dominant positions of distinction, *economically*, in terms of the labour market opportunities they are able to offer and *socially*, through the ways in which they tend to play host to 'groups who are in some way marginalized from the fabric of mainstream society' (Andrews and Roberts, 2012: 3).

First, the places where organizations are *physically* located are integral to how they are socially constructed and understood (Massey, 1994). Organizations become bound up with the layers of history that have accumulated within their physical surroundings: as Orley describes, 'Places retain the traces of what has happened there. However much a wall is whitewashed, evidence of previous activity remains underneath' (2012: 37). While the identities and meanings of place can never be fixed or stable (Massey, 1994), 'its connections, what surrounds it, what formed it, what happened there' (Lippard, 1997:7) define what is special about a place (Massey, 2005). Organizations have long recognized the resources offered by place and space (Dale and Burrell, 2008), with corporate powerhouses jostling for city-centre locations, landmark monuments or regenerated riversides to construct and symbolize their identities. The headquarters of Global Accountants are a good example of this: based in prestigious, high-rise, glass-fronted offices overlooking the River Thames in the heart of London's Central Business District. In contrast, organizations emplaced in declining landscapes offer very different phenomenological and imaginative experiences (Lefebvre, 1991; Brown, 1997). We have described, in our case studies in Glasgow and the North East, how the young people in our research are often trained or offered work placements within organizations situated in urban locations suffering from industrial decline and associated degeneration. This physical positioning on the margins of more centralized and successful sites of urban power is an interconnecting and active process, positioning the young people on the borderlands of mainstream activity, potentially limiting their ability to translate their experiences into other jobs, sectors and places in a competitive regional labour market. On the other hand, we also saw how transformation is possible, with regeneration opening up some new local opportunities in creative ways.

Second, and attendant to this, are the *cultural* resources offered by many organizations involved in youth employability. We have shown that these are very often located in the third sector, itself oft positioned as liminal and intermediate to the public and private sectors, simultaneously reliant on the state for funding and on the private for management techniques (Evers, 1995; Lewis, 1999). At best understood as a hybrid of both sectors (Billis, 2010), at worse they are 'the poor relation', neither one nor the other. As such, work experience gained within the sector is not always perceived as valuable by another. Further, the uneven geographical distribution of cultural capital means, for example, that a small second-hand charity shop in a deprived metropolitan suburb not only occupies a marginal positioning in relation to the hegemonic spaces of retail malls selling luxury goods (Crewe, 2000), but is also a very different cultural landscape from a large charity headquarters located in the city centre. However, the consequences of this liminality are also ambiguous, on the one hand potentially restricting the cultural resources and subjectivities available to young people, and on the other, as we have seen from our case studies in Glasgow and the South Coast, offering new psychic possibilities that may act as a seedbed for cultural creativity, whereby former learner identities based on failure and 'old perspectives on work and subjectivity are contested and new ones created' (Garsten, 1999: 601).

Third, similarly wide discrepancies are found in the *economic* outcomes delivered by different sectors and organizations. To reframe the previous point, in terms of training and career opportunities, as well as pay and conditions, a small community organization in an economically depressed urban suburb occupies a marginal economic position in relation to large charity, public sector and corporate organizations. For trainers as well as trainees, economic security may be elusive. Many within the employability training workforce rely on short-term funding, whether from government, local government or the EU, and may never quite know whether, or for how long, their projects will run. This means their own employment is uncertain and unfixed (Spyridakis, 2013), and may also be temporary, even unpaid and non-standard in terms of conditions of work (UK Voluntary Sector Workforce Almanac, 2013). They too, therefore, may well be in limbo. Many of the young people we met across the case study sites were also juggling constant uncertainty: living in a back-and forth context of temporary/ under- or unemployment, often with minimal support from the local Jobcentre. Constantly experiencing the paradox of not being able to secure a job while spending much of their lives looking for one, they are unable to develop any form of consistent work identity (Spyridakis, 2013). However, the imagination of new work subjectivities and the performance of new skills provided by volunteering programmes were important steps forward for the young people in the transition from economic liminality (Ibarra and Barbulescu, 2010). As we have demonstrated, trainers are often highly skilled in reframing previous experiences, often positioned by the young people themselves as worthless, as incorporating valuable skills by which to realize future work-based ambitions. For these to be achieved in practice, however, an integrated approach of employer engagement is needed, whereby employability organizations not only provide young people with the context and support to practise and augment their skills, but also offer a variety of entry route schemes into paid work for young people at different positions within the youth labour market (Adam et al, 2017).

The physical, cultural and economic locations of employability organizations are often a contingency of their core *social* function of welfare delivery to hard-to-reach groups (Macmillan, 2010; DWP, 2011). In terms of progress into paid work, it is members of this group who are at most risk of long-term liminality (Furlong, 2006). For some young people, liminality becomes a stable, permanent condition, turning into long-term structural exclusion (MacDonald, 2011). For the transitional phase between education and employment to be more successfully negotiated, the transformative potential of liminality (Thomassen, 2012) is a resource that should be intelligently managed by both employers and policy makers.

Risk

The consequences of both social inequality and liminality, in its varied formations, is a greater exposure to, and decreased ability to cope with, risk. Beck (1992a, b; Beck and Beck-Gernsheim, 2002) argues that in a risk society, risk is increasingly significant for determining social groups. This occurs as identification with traditional classes lessens, in favour of increasing individualization and the crafting of self-biographies, so that class and structure are less significant than in past generations. In contrast, Furlong and Cartmel (2007) maintain that class persists as an important determining factor in life chances, and our research certainly highlights the interplay between social inequality, liminality and risk. Wealth offers considerable capacity to prepare and weather activities and situations that present risk, while the lack of material and social resources limits willingness and ability to manage risk. As Giddens (1990, 1991) argued, for those with greater levels of insecurity, making sense of progression pathways that are less clear requires the creation of a reflexive self to shape disparate activities into rational and purposive choices. This aligns well with our post-Foucauldian analytical frame, which has sought to describe and understand how participants' subjective beings are produced through a variety of technologies of governance (Rose, 1989).

In both the North East and in Glasgow, programme trainers spent considerable time with participants to help them identify their skills and interests, and how these could apply to a particular field of work that the young person would enjoy.

In short, they were actively engaging the young people in the aforementioned reflexive self, helping them to become calculated individuals whose previous actions and gained attributes become marketable (Martin, 1997). The participants were then seeking to capitalize on the professional networks of the two programme provider charities through the acquisition of an unpaid work or volunteering placement. The risk for them is that the time commitment of these activities leads nowhere, or to a position that only entrenches their liminality rather than offers a chance to get in and get on in their chosen field. Although both programmes pay expenses during the course and the placements, and therefore do not necessarily increase any risk for the young people, they do not offer any route to security. It is telling and saddening that the main highlight for the young people on both these programmes was the attention that they received from the trainers: for the most vulnerable this was their first taste of support and encouragement.

In contrast, those young people who had secured blue-chip internships that led to graduate employment were offered a secure future, with a clear path both to enter the labour market and progress in their careers. This intervention is characterized by the considerable investment by employers in identifying and growing a talent pool of young people. For those in other fields, internships were a far less secure route, with several of our participants deciding that they were not worth their time and energy. Access to the better internships, in our sample, was considerably mediated by class and social capital.

Our research on the South Coast revealed stark discourses regarding risk. By seeking to establish their own businesses and create their own jobs, both the participants from EY and SEU took on all the risk of their ventures. The different articulations of risk by the two supporting institutions were similarly mediated by the perceived safety-nets accessible to participants. Risk and failure were encouraged in the students who could finance their efforts via student loans, while the long-term unemployed were cautioned against ventures that were not meticulously planned and researched due to their lack of any contingencies. Individualized biographies and responsibilization leads to individualized risk, and this is compounded by social inequality, which in turn correlates with spatial, cultural and economic liminality. Discourses about young people and employability conceal and mask these elements as policy makers, supporting organizations and young people internalize the view that progression into the labour market relies on the activities of the individual.

Fit for the future?

We have discussed in this book how various social theorists of advanced modernization have explored the impacts of social and economic change on the production of the self. In brief, the argument of theorists such as Beck, Bauman and Giddens is that globalization and neoliberalism have transformed understandings of the self, as traditional forms of social life have come under scrutiny, exposed to the transformational impact not only of free-market logic but also the development of technology, communications and informational frameworks (Elliott, 2019). Although we have not discussed the latter aspects in this book, they certainly deserve fuller attention in future research. Work futures analysts argue that we are in the midst of a digital revolution, a 'fourth industrial revolution' (Elliott, 2019), bringing along with it changes in established skills, jobs and workplaces, sometimes in dramatic and unanticipated ways. Digital skills are becoming more and more essential, not only to get into employment, but certainly to get on and progress, possibly in a whole range of as yet undefined future careers. Yet we did not find that digital skills – and the affordances that these could offer to young people – featured significantly in any of our ethnographies. The skills that young people were being trained in were, by and large, the quite traditional ones of face-to-face communication, teamwork, time keeping, literacy and numeracy, and so on. These skills are undeniably important: indeed, for some thinkers such as Colvin (2015), it is these very skills that will *gain* in importance if automation takes over many routine jobs. However, at the same time, the curriculums of employability programmes need to acknowledge the changing employment picture and be more forward thinking about the skills promoted. Trainers – and young people – need to be well prepared for the future, and for the fact that it may change in unpredictable ways, creating new demands for very different kinds of work and very different sorts of skills. Without this, the disadvantages of social inequality, liminality and risk that we have identified will be further exacerbated by lack of fitness for future labour markets.

References

Adam, D., Atfield, G. and Green, A. (2017) 'What works? Policies for employability in cities', *Urban Studies*, 54(5): 1162–77.

Adkins, L. (2015) 'Disobedient workers, the law and the making of unemployment markets', *Sociology*, 51(2): 290–305.

Adonis, A. (2013) *North East Independent Economic Review*, North East Local Enterprise Partnership, https://www.thenorthernecho.co.uk/resources/files/28979

Ahl, H. (2006) 'Why research on women entrepreneurs needs new directions', *Entrepreneurship Theory and Practice,* 30(5): 595–621.

Ainley, P. (2016) *Betraying a Generation: How Education is Failing Young People*, Bristol: Policy Press.

Alcock, P. (2012) 'New policy spaces: the impact of devolution on third sector policy in the UK', *Social Policy and Administration*, 46(2): 219–38.

Allen, K., Quinn, J. Hollingsworth, S. and Rose, A. (2013) 'Becoming employable students and "ideal" creative workers: exclusion and inequality in higher education work placements', *British Journal of the Sociology of Education*, 34(3): 431–52.

Anderson, P. and Green, P. (2012) 'Beyond CV building: the communal benefits of student volunteering', *Voluntary Sector Review*, 3(2): 247–56.

Andrews, H. and Roberts, L. (eds) (2012) *Liminal Landscapes: Travel, Experience and Spaces In-between*, London: Routledge.

Ashley, L. and Empson, L. (2013) 'Differentiation and discrimination: understanding social class and social exclusion in leading law firms', *Human Relations*, 66(2): 219–44.

Ashley, L. and Empson, L. (2016) 'Understanding social exclusion in elite professional service firms: field level dynamics and 'the professional project', *Work, Employment and Society*, 3(2): 211–29.

Athayde, R. (2009) 'Measuring enterprise potential in young people', *Entrepreneurship Theory and Practice*, 33(2): 481–500.

Babb, P. (2005) *Measurement of Social Capital in the UK*, London: ONS.

Ball, J., Milano, D. and Ferguson, B. (2012) 'Half of UK's young black males are unemployed', *The Guardian*, 9 March, www.theguardian.com/society/2012/mar/09/half-uk-young-black-men-unemployed

Ball, S., Maguire, M. and Macrae, S. (2000) *Choice, Pathways and Transitions Post-16: New Youth, New Economies in the Global Society*, London: Routledge.

Ball, S.J. (2013) *The Education Debate* (2nd edn), Bristol: Policy Press.

Baudrillard, J. (1988) *Selected Writings*, Mark Poster (ed), Cambridge: Polity Press.

Bauman, Z. (2000) *Liquid Modernity*, Cambridge: Polity Press.

Baxter, J. (2003) *Positioning Gender in Discourse: A Feminist Methodology*, Basingstoke: Palgrave Macmillan.

Beck, U. (1992a) 'From industrial society to the risk society: questions of survival, social structure and ecological enlightenment', *Theory, Culture & Society*, 9(1): 97–123.

Beck, U. (1992b) *Risk Society: Towards a New Modernity*, London: Sage Publications.

Beck, U. and Beck-Gernsheim, E. (2002) *Individualization: Institutionalized Individualism and its Social and Political Consequences*, London, Thousand Oaks, CA: Sage Publications.

BEIS (Department for Business, Energy and Industrial Strategy) (2017) *Industrial Strategy: Building a Britain Fit for the Future*, www.gov.uk/government/publications/industrial-strategy-building-a-britain-fit-for-the-future

Bell, D. and Blanchflower, D. (2010) 'UK unemployment in the great recession', *National Institute Economic Review*, 214(1): 3–25.

Bell, D. and Blanchflower, D. (2011) 'Young people and the great recession', *Oxford Review of Economic Policy*, 27(2): 241–67.

Bennet, M. and Parameshwaran, M. (2013) *What Factors Predict Volunteering among Youth in the UK?*, Briefing Paper 102, Birmingham: Third Sector Research Centre, University of Birmingham.

Billis, D. (2010) *Hybrid Organisations and the Third Sector: Challenges for Practice, Theory and Policy*, Basingstoke: Palgrave Macmillan.

Blatterer, H. (2010a) 'The changing semantics of youth and adulthood', *Cultural Sociology*, 4(1): 63–79.

Blatterer, H. (2010b) 'Generations, modernity and the problem of contemporary adulthood', in J. Burnett (ed) *Contemporary Adulthood: Calendars, Cartographies and Constructions,* Basingstoke: Palgrave Macmillan, pp. 10–23.

Bögenhold, D. and Klinglmair, A. (2015) 'Female solo self-employment-features of gendered entrepreneurship', *International Review of Entrepreneurship*, 13(1): 47–58.

Borlagdan, J. (2015) 'Inequality and 21-year-olds' negotiation of uncertain transition to employment: a Bourdieusian approach', *Journal of Youth Studies*, 18(7): 839–54.

Born, G. (2004) *Uncertain Vision: Birt, Dyke and the Reinvention of the BBC*, London: Martin Secker & Warburg Ltd.

Brewis, G., Russell, J. and Holsworth, C. (2010) *Bursting the Bubble: Students, Volunteering and the Community Research Summary*, www.publicengagement.ac.uk/sites/default/files/publication/nccpe_bursting_the_bubble_fullreport_0_0.pdf

Bright Network (nd) 'What are the differences between the Big Four accountancy firms?', www.brightnetwork.co.uk/career-path-guides/accounting-audit-tax/differences-big-four-firms

Brinkley, I., Jones, K. and Lee, N. (2013) *The Gender Jobs Split*, London: Touchstone Publications.

Britton, J., Dearden, L., Shephard, N. and Vignoles, A. (2016) *How English Domiciled Graduate Earnings Vary with Gender, Institution Attended, Subject and Socio-Economic Background*, IFS Working Paper W16/06, London: Institute for Fiscal Studies.

Brooks, R. (2007) 'Young people's extra-curricular activities: critical social engagement – or "something for the CV"?', *Journal of Social Policy*, 36(3): 417–34.

Brooks, R. (2009) 'Young people and political participation: an analysis of European Union policies', *Sociological Research Online*, 14(1).

Brooks, R. (2017) 'The construction of higher education students in English policy documents', *British Journal of Sociology of Education*, 39(6): 745–61.

Brooks, R. and Everett, G. (2009) 'Post graduation reflections on the value of a degree', *British Educational Research Journal*, 35(3): 333–49.

Brown, G., Krafti, P., Pickerill, J. and Upton, C. (2012) 'Holding the future together: towards a theorisation of the spaces and times of transition', *Environment and Planning A*, 44: 1607–23.

Brown, J. (2013) *Southampton's Changing Faces*, Nottingham: JMD Media/DB Publishing.

Brown, M. (1997) *RePlacing Citizenship: AIDS Activism and Radical Democracy*, New York: Guilford Press.

Brown, P. (2013) 'Education, opportunity and the prospects for social mobility', *British Journal of Social Mobility*, 34(5–6): 678–700.

Brown, P. and Lauder, H. (2001) *Capitalism and Social Progress: The Future of Society in a Global Economy*, Basingstoke: Palgrave Macmillan.

Bruni, A., Gherardi, S. and Poggio, B. (2004) 'Doing gender, doing entrepreneurship: an ethnographic account of intertwined practices', *Gender, Work & Organization,* 11(4): 406–29.

Bunk, J.A., Dugan, A.G., D'Agostino, A.L. and Barnes-Farrell, J.L. (2012) 'Understanding work-to-family conflict among self-employed workers: utilising a cognitive appraisal framework', *The Journal of Entrepreneurship*, 21(2): 223–51.

Burchardt, T. (2005) *The Education and Employment of Disabled Young People*, Joseph Rowntree Foundation, www.jrf.org.uk/report/education-and-employment-disabled-young-people

Butler, S. (2018) 'Initiative to crack down on unpaid internships launched in the UK', *The Guardian*, 8 February, www.theguardian.com/society/2018/feb/08/initiative-to-crack-down-on-unpaid-internships-launched-in-uk

Bynner, J. (2013) 'School to work transitions and wellbeing in a changing labour market', in H. Helve and K. Evans (eds) *Youth and Work Transitions in Changing Social Landscapes*, London: Tufnell Press, pp. 31–44.

Cabinet Office (2014) *Fair Access to Professional Careers* https://assets. publishing.service.gov.uk/government/uploads/system/uploads/ attachment_data/file/61090/IR_FairAccess_acc2.pdf

Cabinet Office (2018) *Civil Society Strategy: Building a Future that Works for Everyone*, https://assets.publishing.service.gov.uk/government/ uploads/system/uploads/attachment_data/file/732765/Civil_ Society_Strategy_-_building_a_future_that_works_for_everyone. pdf

Caird, S. (1990) 'Enterprise education: the need for differentiation', *British Journal of Education & Work*, 4(1): 47–57.

Cameron, D. (2011). 'Speech to Conservative Spring Conference', *New Statesman*, 6 March, www.newstatesman.com/2011/03/ enterprise-government-party

Carers Trust (nd) 'Key facts about carers and the people they care for', https://carers.org/key-facts-about-carers-and-people-they-care

CIPD (Chartered Institute of Personnel and Development) (2010) *Learning and Talent Development: Annual Survey Report 2010*, London: CIPD.

Cohen, L. and Musson, G. (2000) 'Entrepreneurial identities: reflections from two case studies', *Organization*, 7(1): 31–48.

Cohen, P. and Ainley P. (2000) 'In the country of the blind? Youth studies and cultural studies in Britain', *Journal of Youth Studies*, 3(1): 79–95.

Colvin, G. (2015) *Humans are Underrrated: What High Achievers Know that Brilliant Machines Never Will*, London: Nicholas Brealey Publishing.

Conroy, M. (1975) *Regional Economic Diversification*, New York, NY: Praeger.

Corrigan, T. (2015) 'Media and cultural industries internships: a thematic review and digital labour parallels', *tripleC*, 13(2): 336–50.

Coslett, R. (2015) 'Too little, too late: unpaid internships only widen the gap between rich and poor', *New Statesman*, 17 April, www. newstatesman.com/politics/2015/04/too-little-too-late-unpaid-internships-only-widen-appalling-gap-between-rich-and

Crewe, L. (2000) 'Geographies of retailing and consumption', *Progress in Human Geography*, 24(2): 275–90.

Crisp, R. and Powell, R. (2017) 'Young people and UK labour market policy: a critique of "employability" as a tool for understanding youth unemployment', *Urban Studies*, 54(8): 1784–807.

Crosnoe, R. (2014) 'Youth, economic hardship, and the worldwide Great Recession', *Longitudinal and Life Course Studies*, 5(2): 199–204.

Crossley, L. (2014) 'The school leavers who aren't ready for work: one in three business executives are concerned about young people's attitude', *Daily Mail*, 4 July, www.dailymail.co.uk/news/article-2680331/The-school-leavers-arent-ready-work-One-three-business-executives-concerned-young-peoples-attitude.html#ixzz5GVHsdruy

Crouch, D. (2012) 'Afterword', in H. Andrews and L. Roberts (eds) *Liminal Landscapes: Travel, Experience and Spaces In-Between*, London: Routledge, pp. 234–41.

Crowley, L. and Cominetti, N. (2014) *The Geography of Youth Unemployment: A Route Map for Change*, www.theworkfoundation.com/DownloadPublication/Report/360_The%20Geography%20of%20Youth%20Unemployment%20FINAL%2008%2004%2014.pdf

Curran, J. and Blackburn, R.A. (1990) 'Youth and the enterprise culture', *British Journal of Education & Work*, 4(1): 31–45.

Dale, K. and Burrell, G. (2008) *The Spaces of Organization and The Organization of Space*, Basingstoke: Palgrave Macmillan.

Danson, M. (2005) 'Old industrial regions and employability', *Urban Studies*, 42(2): 285–300.

Davis Smith, J. with Howlett, S. (2003) *Towards a Global Research Agenda on Civic Service: An International Conference Draft Paper on Western Europe*, London: Institute for Volunteering Research.

Dean, J. (2013) 'Manufacturing citizens: the dichotomy between policy and practice in youth volunteering in the UK', *Administrative Theory and Practice*, 35(1): 46–62.

Dean, J. (2014) 'How structural factors promote instrumental motivations within youth volunteering: a qualitative analysis of volunteer brokerage', *Voluntary Sector Review*, 5(2): 231–47.

Dean, J. (2015) 'Volunteering, the market and neoliberalism', *People, Place and Policy*, 9(2): 139–14.

Deetz, S. (1998) 'Discursive formations, strategized subordination and self-surveillance', in A. McKinlay and K. Starkey (eds) *Foucault, Management and Organization Theory: From Panopticon to Technologies of Self* (1st edn), London and Thousand Oaks, CA: Sage Publications, pp. 151–72.

Devins, D. and Hogarth, T. (2005) 'Employing the unemployed: some case study evidence on the role and practice of employers', *Urban Studies*, 42(2): 245–56.

DirectGov (2016) 'Work experience and volunteering', https://www.gov.uk/moving-from-benefits-to-work/work-experience-and-volunteering

Donnan, A. and Carthy, R. (2011) *Graduate Employment and Internships: Issues from the Environmental Sciences and Sustainability Sectors*, London: Institution of Environmental Sciences.

Donnelly, M. and Evans, C. (2016) 'Framing the geographies of higher education participation: schools, place and national identity', *British Educational Research Journal*, 42(1): 74–92.

Du Bois-Reymond, M. (1998) ' "I don't want to commit myself yet": young people's life concepts', *Journal of Youth Studies*, 1(1): 63–79.

DWP (Department for Work and Pensions) Welfare to Work and Equality Group (2009) *The Six Month Offer Support for Newly Unemployed and Six Month Offer Evaluations: A Report on Qualitative Research Findings?* www.gov.uk/government/publications/support-for-newly-unemployed-and-six-month-offer-evaluations-a-reporton-qualitative-research-findings-rr691

DWP (2011) *The Work Programme*, London: DWP.

DWP (2012) *Get Britain Working: Work Together*, https://webarchive.nationalarchives.gov.uk/20130125100825/http://www.dwp.gov.uk/docs/work-together-lft.pdf

Dyck, I. (2005) 'Feminist geography, the "everyday", and local-global relations: hidden spaces of place-making', *The Canadian Geographer*, 49(3): 233–43.

Edwards, R. and Usher, R. (1994) 'Disciplining the subject: the power of competence', *Studies in the Education of Adults*, 35(1): 54–69.

Eisenstadt, S. (1956) *From Generation to Generation: Age Groups and Social Structure*, Piscataway, NJ: Transaction Publishers.

Elden, S. (2007) 'Rethinking governmentality', *Political Geography*, 26(1): 29–33.

Elliott, A. (2019) *The Culture of AI: Everyday Life and the Digital Revolution*, London: Routledge.

Ellis Paine, A., McKay, S. and Moro, D. (2013) 'Does volunteering improve employability? Insights from the British household panel survey and beyond', *Voluntary Sector Review*, 9(4): 355–76.

EU (European Union) (2013) *Council Recommendation of 22 April 2013 on Establishing a Youth Guarantee*, https://eur-lex.europa.eu/legal-content/EN/ALL/?uri=CELEX:32013H0426(01)

European Commission (2004) *Action Plan: The European Agenda for Entrepreneurship*, https://ec.europa.eu/growth/smes/promoting-entrepreneurship/action-plan_en

European Commission (2013) *EU Commission 2020 Action Plan Reigniting the Entrepreneurial Spirit in Europe*, https://eur-lex.europa.eu/legal-content/EN/TXT/HTML/?uri=CELEX:52012DC0795&from=EN

European Commission (2015) *EU Youth Report 2015*, http://ec.europa.eu/assets/eac/youth/library/reports/youth-report-2015_en.pdf

European Commission (nd[a]) *The Youth Guarantee*, https://ec.europa.eu/social/main.jsp?catId=1079&langId=en

European Commission (nd[b]) *Youth Employment Initiative*, https://ec.europa.eu/social/main.jsp?catId=1176&langId=en

Evans, J. (2013) *Youth Contract*, Commons Briefing Papers SN06387, London: House of Commons Library. http://researchbriefings.files.parliament.uk/documents/SN06387/SN06387.pdf

Evans, K. (2002) 'Taking control of their lives? Agency in young adult transitions in England and the new Germany', *Journal of Youth Studies*, 5(3): 245–69.

Evers, A. (1995) 'Part of the welfare mix: The third sector as an intermediate area', *Voluntas*, 6(2): 159–82.

EY Foundation (2016) *The Employment Landscape for Young People in the UK: Challenges and Opportunities*, London: Ernst and Young LLP.

Felstead, A., Gallic, D., Green, F. and Henseke, G. (2018) *Insecurity at Work in Britain: First Findings from the Skills and Employment Survey 2017*, Project Report, London: Centre for Learning and Life Chances in Knowledge Economies and Societies, UCL Institute of Education.

Fergusson, R. (2013) 'Against disengagement: non-participation as an object of governance', *Research in Post-Compulsory Education*, 18(1–2): 12–28.

Field, J. (2000) *Lifelong Learning and the New Educational Order*, Stoke-on-Trent: Trentham Books.

Figiel, J. (2013) 'Work experience without qualities? A documentary and critical account of an internship', *Ephemera Theory and Politics in Organization*, 13(1): 33–52.

Finn, D. (2000) 'From full employment to employability: a new deal for Britain's unemployed?', *International Journal of Manpower*, 21(5): 384–99.

Finn, D. and Simmonds, D. (2003) *Intermediate Labour Market in Britain and an International Review of Transitional Employment Programme*, London: Department for Work and Pensions.

Foucault, M. (1980) *Power/Knowledge*, Brighton: Harvester Press.

Foucault, M. (2003) 'Governmentality', in P. Rabinow and N. Rose (eds) *The Essential Foucault: Selections from Essential Works of Foucault 1954–1984*, London: The New Press, pp. 229–45.

Foucault, M. (2007) *Security, Territory, Population*, Basingstoke: Palgrave Macmillan.

France, A. (2016) *Understanding Youth in the Global Economic Crisis*, Bristol: Policy Press.

France, A. and Roberts, S. (2015) 'The problem of social generations: a critique of the new emerging orthodoxy in youth studies', *Journal of Youth Studies*, 18(2): 215–30.

France, A. and Roberts, S. (2017) *Youth and Social Class: Enduring Inequality in the United Kingdom, Australia and New Zealand*, London: Palgrave Macmillan.

Francis-Devine, F. (2015) *Youth Unemployment Statistics*, Briefing Paper Number 5871, House of Commons Library, https://researchbriefings.parliament.uk/ResearchBriefing/Summary/SN05871

Frenette, A. (2013) 'Making the intern economy: role and career challenges of the music industry intern,' *Work and Occupations*, 40(4): 364–97.

Fuller, A., Unwin, L., Guile, D. and Rizvi, S. (2010) *Economic Regeneration, Social Cohesion, and the Welfare-to-Work Industry: Innovation, Opportunity and Compliance in the City-Region*, LLAKES Research Paper 7, Southampton: Centre for Learning and Life Chances in Knowledge Economies and Societies.

Furlong, A. (2006) 'Not a very NEET solution: representing problematic labour market transitions among early school leavers', *Work Employment and Society*, 20(3): 553–69.

Furlong, A. and Cartmel, F. (2007) *Young People and Social Change: New Perspectives*, Maidenhead: Open University Press.

Furlong, A., Goodwin, J., O'Connor, H., Hadfield, S., Hall, S., Lowden, K. and Plugor, R. (2018) *Young People in the Labour Market: Past, Present and Future*, London: Routledge.

Garsten, C. (1999) 'Betwixt and between: temporary employees as liminal subjects in flexible organizations', *Organization Studies*, 20(4): 601–17.

Garsten, C. and Jacobsson, K. (2003) *Learning to be Employable: New Agendas on Work, Responsibility and Learning in a Globalizing World*, Basingstoke: Palgrave Macmillan.

Gaskin, K. (2004) *Young People, Volunteering and Civic Service: A Review of the Literature*, London: Institute for Volunteering Research.

GCPP (Glasgow Community Planning Partnership) (2013) *Glasgow's Single Outcome Agreement 2013*, www.glasgowcpp.org.uk/CHttpHandler.ashx?id=15989&p=0

Giddens, A. (1990) *The Consequences of Modernity*, Cambridge: Polity Press.

Giddens, A. (1991) *Modernity and Self-identity: Self and Society in the Late Modern Age*, Palo Alto, CA: Stanford University Press.

Giorgi, G. de (2005) *Long-Term Effects of a Mandatory Multistage Program: The New Deal for Young People in the UK*, IFS Working Paper WP05/08, www.ifs.org.uk/wps/wp0508.pdf

Gledhill, J. (2004) 'Neoliberalism', in D. Nugent and J. Vincent Malden (eds) *A Companion to the Anthropology of Politics*, Oxford: Wiley-Blackwell, pp. 332–48.

Glucksmann, M. (2000) *Cottons and Casuals: The Gendered Organization of Labour in Time and Space*, Durham: Sociology Press.

Glucksmann, M. (2005) 'Shifting boundaries and interconections', in L. Pettinger, R. Parry Taylor and M. Glucksmann (eds) *A New Sociology of Work?*, Oxford: Blackwell Publishing/The Sociological Review, pp. 19–36.

Gomez, M. (1998) 'Reflective images: the case of urban regeneration in Glasgow and Bilbao', *International Journal of Urban and Regional Research*, 22(1): 106–21.

Goodwin, J. and O'Connor, H. (2005) 'Exploring complex transitions: looking back on the 'golden age' of from school to work', *Sociology*, 39(2): 201–20.

GOV.UK (2017) 'Unpaid internships are damaging to social mobility', www.gov.uk/government/news/unpaid-internships-are-damaging-to-social-mobility

GOV.UK (2018a) 'The UK's Industrial Strategy', www.gov.uk/government/topical-events/the-uks-industrial-strategy

GOV.UK (2018b) 'Unemployment', www.ethnicity-facts-figures.service.gov.uk/work-pay-and-benefits/unemployment-and-economic-inactivity/unemployment/latest

Grabher, G. (2004) 'Learning in projects, remembering in networks? Communality, sociality, and connectivity in project ecologies', *European Urban and Regional Studies*, 11(2): 103–23.

Graeber, D. (2009) 'Neoliberalism, or the bureaucratization of the world', in H. Gusterson and C. Besteman (eds) *The Insecure American: How We Got Here and What We Should Do About It*, Oakland, CA: University of California Press, pp. 79–98.

Grant-Smith, D. and McDonald, P. (2016) 'The trend toward pre-graduation professional work experience for Australian young planners: essential experience or essentially exploitation', *Australian Planner*, 53(2): 65–72.

Grant-Smith, D. and McDonald, P. (2018) 'Ubiquitous yet ambiguous: an integrative review of unpaid work', *International Journal of Management Review*, 20(20): 559–78.

Green, A. (2017) *The Crisis for Young People: Generational Inequalities in Education, Work, Housing and Welfare*, Cham: Palgrave Macmillan.

Green, A., Atfield, G. and Purcell, K. (2015) 'Fuelling displacement and labour market segmentation in low-skilled jobs? Insights from a local study of migrant and student employment', *Environment and Planning A*, 48(3): 577–93.

Green, E. and Cohen, L. (1995) ' "Women's business": are women entrepreneurs breaking new ground or simply balancing the demands of "women's work" in a new way?', *Journal of Gender Studies*, 4(3): 297–314.

Green, F. (2013) *Youth Entrepreneurship*, www.oecd.org/cfe/leed/youth_bp_finalt.pdf

Green, F., Felstead, A. and Gallie, D. (2016) 'Job quality and inequality: the unequal world of work in the UK, 1986–2012', *Juncture*, 22(4): 329–33.

Greene, F. J. and Storey, D. J. (2005) *Evaluating Youth Entrepreneurship: The Case of The Prince's Trust*. Centre for Small and Medium Sized Enterprises, Warwick Business School, http://www.mbsportal.bl.uk/secure/subjareas/smlbusentrep/wubs/csmsewp/124719wp88.pdf

Gregson, N. and Crewe L. (2003) *Second-hand Cultures*, Oxford: Berg.

Guile, D. and Lahiff, A. (2013) *Internship: Conventional Wisdom, Models and Recommendations*, LLAKES Research Papers, University of London: Institute of Education, https://www.srhe.ac.uk/downloads/events/114_Internship.pdf

Halabisky, D., Potter, J., Greene, F., European Commission, Directorate-General for Employment, and Organisation for Economic Co-operation and Development (2012) *Policy Brief on Youth Entrepreneurship: Entrepreneurial Activities in Europe*, Luxembourg: Publications Office of the European Union. https://www.oecd.org/employment/leed/Youth%20entrepreneurship%20policy%20brief%20EN_FINAL.pdf

Halford, S. and Leonard, P. (2001) *Gender, Power and Organisation,* Basingstoke: Palgrave Macmillan.

Halford, S., Leonard, P. and Bruce, K. (2015) 'Geographies of labour in the third sector: making hybrid workforces in place', *Environment and Planning A*, 47(11): 2355–72.

Harari, D. (2011) *Future Jobs Fund*, Commons Briefing Papers SN05352, https://researchbriefings.parliament.uk/ResearchBriefing/Summary/SN05352

Harvey, D. (2005) *A Brief History of Neoliberalism*, Oxford: Oxford University Press.

Harvey, L. (2003) 'Employability and diversity', www2.wlv.ac.uk/webteam/confs/socdiv/sdd-harvey-0602.doc

HEFCE (Higher Education Funding Council for England) (2011) *Increasing Opportunities for High-Quality HE Work Experience*, Careers Research and Advisory Centre, https://webarchive.nationalarchives.gov.uk/20180319115421/http://www.hefce.ac.uk/pubs/rereports/year/2011/highqualheworkexp/

Heinz, W. (2009) 'Youth transitions in an age of uncertainty', in A. Furlong (ed) *Handbook of Youth and Young Adulthood*, Abingdon: Routledge, pp. 3–13.

Heinz, W. (2014) 'Did the Great Recession affect young people's aspirations and reinforce social inequality?', *Longitudinal and Life Course Studies*, 5(2): 189–98

Helve, H. and Evans, K. (2013) *Youth and Work Transitions in Changing Social Landscapes*, London: Tufnell Press.

Hesmondhalgh, D. (2010) 'User-generated content, free labour and the cultural industries', *Ephemera*, 10(3–4): 267–84.

Hilbrecht, M. and Lero, D.S. (2014) 'Self-employment and family life: constructing work–life balance when you're "always on"', *Community, Work & Family*, 17(1): 20–42.

Hillage, J. and Pollard, E. (1998) *Employability: Developing a Framework for Policy Analysis*, Research Brief 85, London: Department for Education and Employment.

Hillmore, A., Lally, J., Marlow, S., Prince, S. and Pritchard, D. (2012) *Early Impacts of Mandatory Work Activity*, Department for Work and Pensions, https://assets.publishing.service.gov.uk/government/uploads/system/uploads/attachment_data/file/222938/early_impacts_mwa.pdf

HM Government (2011) *Supporting Youth Employment: An Overview of the Coalition Government's Approach*, London: HM Government.

Hodge, S. and Harris, R. (2012) 'Discipline, governmentality and 25 years of competency-based training', *Studies in the Education of Adults*, 44(2): 155–70.

Hodgson, C. and Charles, D. (nd) *Case Study North East England (UK)*. Contract No. 2008.CE.16.0.AT.020. Regional Policy Development Evaluation Unit. European Commisssion. https://ec.europa.eu/regional_policy/sources/docgener/evaluation/pdf/expost2006/wp4_final_report_p1_en.pdf

Holdsworth, C. and Quinn, J. (2010) 'Student volunteering in English higher education', *Studies in Higher Education*, 35(1): 113–27.

Hoskins, B., Leonard, P. and Wilde, R.J. (2017) 'Negotiating uncertain economic times: youth employment strategies in England', *British Educational Research Journal*, 44(1): 61–79.

House of Commons Work and Pensions Committee (2010) *Youth Unemployment and the Future Jobs Fund*, https://publications.parliament.uk/pa/cm201011/cmselect/cmworpen/472/472.pdf

House of Commons Work and Pensions Committee (2012) *Youth Unemployment and the Youth Contract*, HC 151, House of Commons, https://publications.parliament.uk/pa/cm201213/cmselect/cmworpen/151/151.pdf

Houston, D. (2005) 'Employability, skills mismatch and spatial mismatch in metropolitan labour markets', *Urban Studies*, 42 (2): 221–43.

Howard-Grenville, J., Golden-Biddle, K., Irwin, J. and Mao, J. (2011) 'Liminality as cultural process for cultural change', *Organization Science*, 22(2): 522–39.

Howker, E. and Malik, S. (2010) *Jilted Generation: How Britain has Bankrupted its Youth*, London: Icon Books.

Hustinx, L. (2001) 'Individualisation and new styles of volunteering: an empirical exploration', *Voluntary Action*, 3(2): 57–76.

Ibarra, H. and Barbulescu, R. (2010) 'Identity as narrative: prevalence, effectiveness, and consequences of narrative identity work in macro-work role transitions', *Academy of Management Review*, 35(1): 135–54.

Illgner, A. (2018) 'Why I'm suing over my dream internship', *The Guardian*, 27 March, www.theguardian.com/news/2018/mar/27/why-im-suing-over-my-dream-internship

ILO (International Labour Organization) (2012) *Global Employment Trends*, Geneva: ILO.

Inda, J. (2005) 'Analysis of the modern: an introduction', in J. Inda (ed) *Anthropologies of Modernity: Foucault, Governmentality and Life Politics*, Oxford: Blackwell, pp. 1–20.

IPPR (Institute for Public Policy Research) (2010) *Trends in Part-Time and Temporary Work for the Young*, London: IPPR.

IPPR (2017) *The Inbetweeners: The New Role of Internships in the Graduate Labour Market*, London: IPPR.

Jamieson, L. (2017) 'Migration, place and class: youth in a rural areas', *The Sociological Review*, 48(2): 203–23.

Javid, S. (2016) 'Oral answers to questions: Enterprise Bill', Hansard, House of Commons, 2 February 2016, Column 808, https://publications.parliament.uk/pa/cm201516/cmhansrd/cm160202/debtext/160202-0002.htm#160202-0002.htm_spnew48

Jessop, B. (2002) *The Future of the Capitalist State*, Cambridge: Polity Press.

Johansen, V. (2013) 'Entrepreneurship education and start-up activity: a gender perspective', *International Journal of Gender and Entrepreneurship,* 5(2): 216–31.

Johnson, C. (1988) 'Enterprise education and training', *British Journal of Education & Work,* 2(1): 61–5.

Jones, G. (1999). '"The same people in the same places"? Socio-spatial identities and migration in youth', *Sociology,* 33(1): 001–022.

Jones, G. and Jamieson, L. (1997) *Young People in Rural Scotland: Getting Out and Staying On,* CES Briefing 13, University of Edinburgh: Edinburgh.

Kamerāde, D. and Ellis Paine, A. (2014) 'Volunteering and employability: implications for policy and practice', *Voluntary Sector Review,* 5(2): 259–73.

Kay, T. and Bradbury, S. (2009) 'Youth sport volunteering: developing social capital?', *Sport, Education and Society,* 14(1): 121–40.

Keat, R. and Abercrombie, N. (eds) (1991) *Enterprise Culture,* New York, NY: Routledge.

Lafer, G. (2002) *The Job Training Charade,* Ithaca, NY: Cornell University Press.

Lawton, K. and Potter, D. (2010) *Why Interns Need a Fair Wage,* IPPR and Internocracy, www.ippr.org/publications/why-interns-need-a-fair-wage

Lee, D. (2015) 'Internships, workfare, and the cultural industries: a British perspective', *tripleC,* 13(2): 459–70.

Lee, D. (2018) 'The government wants to stamp out unpaid internships? It could start with the offices of Tory MPs', *New Statesman,* 9 February, www.newstatesman.com/politics/uk/2018/02/unpaid-internships-conservatives-mps-government

Lefebvre, H. (1991) *The Production of Space,* Oxford: Blackwell.

Lemke, T. (2001) '"The birth of bio-politics": Michel Foucault's lecture at the Collège de France on neo-liberal governmentality', *Economy and Society,* 30(2): 190–207.

Leonard, P. (2010) *Expatriate Identities in Postcolonial Organizations: Working Whiteness,* Aldershot: Ashgate.

Leonard, P. (2013) '"The internship": precarious work futures #2', *Work Thought Blog*, https://generic.wordpress.soton.ac.uk/wfrc/2013/07/25/the-internship-precarious-work-futures-2

Leonard, P., Fuller, A. and Unwin, L. (2018) 'A new start? Negotiations of age and chrononormativity by older apprentices in England', *Ageing & Society*, 38(8): 1667–92.

Leonard, P., Halford, S. and Bruce, K. (2016) 'The new degree?' Constructing internships in the third sector', *Sociology*, 50(2): 383–99.

Lewis, J. (1999) 'Reviewing the relationship between the voluntary sector and the state in Britain in the 1990s', *Voluntas*, 10(3): 255–70.

Lindsay, C. and Houston, D. (2011) 'Fit for purpose? Welfare reform and challenges for health and labour market policy in the UK', *Environment and Planning A*, 43(3): 703–21.

Lippard, L. (1997) *The Lure of the Local: Sense of Place in a Multicentred Society*, New York, NY: New York Press.

Lipsky, M. (1980) *Street-Level Bureaucracy: Dilemmas of the Individual in Public Services*, New York, NY: Russell Sage Foundation.

Lister, R., Middleton, S. and Smith, N. (2002) *Young People's Voices: Citizenship Education*, Leicester: National Youth Agency.

London Youth (2018) *Hidden in Plain Sight: Young Londoners Unemployed yet Unsupported*, http://londonyouth.org/wp-content/uploads/2018/05/Hidden-in-Plain-Sight-Web-Version.pdf

Low, N., Butt, S., Ellis Paine, A. and Davis Smith, J. (2007) *Helping Out: A National Survey of Volunteering and Charitable Giving*, London: Cabinet Office.

Low Pay Commission (2011) *National Minimum Wage*, London: Low Pay Commission.

Lyotard, J.-F. (1979) *The Postmodern Condition: A Report on Knowledge*, Manchester: Manchester University Press.

MacDonald, R. (1991) 'Risky business? Youth in the enterprise culture', *Journal of Education Policy*, 6(3): 255–69.

MacDonald, R. (2011) 'Youth transitions, unemployment and under-employment: Plus ça change, plus c'est la même chose?' *Journal of Sociology*, 47(4): 427–44.

MacDonald, R., Shildrick, T., Webster, C. and Simpson, D. (2005) 'Growing up in poor neighbourhoods: the significance of class and place in the extended transitions of "socially excluded" young adults', *Sociology*, 39(5): 873–91.

MacInnes, T., Aldridge, H. and Bushe, S. (2013) *Monitoring Poverty and Social Exclusion*, York: Joseph Rowntree Foundation.

Macmillan, R. (2010) *The Third Sector Delivering Public Services: An Evidence Review*, Third Sector Research Centre Working Paper 20, Birmingham: Third Sector Research Centre, University of Birmingham.

Maelah, R., Mohamed, Z., Ramli, R. and Aman, A. (2014) 'Internship for accounting undergraduates: comparative insights from stakeholders', *Education + Training*, 56(6): 482–502.

Mains, D. (2013) 'Young men's struggle for adulthood in urban Ethiopia', in V. Amit and N. Dyck (eds) *Young Men in Uncertain Times*, New York, NY and Oxford: Berghahn, pp. 110–31.

Manning, N. (2010) 'Tensions in young people's conceptualisation and practice of politics', *Sociological Research Online*, 15(4): 1–10.

Marler, J.H. and Moen, P. (2005) 'Alternative employment arrangements: a gender perspective', *Sex Roles*, 52(5–6): 337–49.

Martin, E. (1997) 'Managing Americans: policy changes and the meanings of work and the self', in C. Shore and S. Wright (eds) *Anthropology of Policy: Critical Perspectives on Governance and Power*, London: Routledge, pp. 183–200.

Martin, R., Sunley, P., Gardiner, B. and Tyler, P. (2016) 'How regions react to recessions: resilience and the role of economic structure', *Regional Studies*, 50(4): 561–85.

Massey, D. (1994) *Space, Place and Gender*, Cambridge: Polity Press.

Massey, D. (2005) *For Space*, London: Sage Publications.

May, T. (2017) 'Theresa May's relaunch speech: full transcript', *The Spectator*, 11 July, https://blogs.spectator.co.uk/2017/07/theresa-mays-relaunch-speech-full-transcript

McDonald, C. and Marston, G. (2005) 'Workfare as welfare: governing unemployment in the advanced liberal state', *Critical Social Policy*, 25(2): 374–401.

McDowell, L. (2002) 'Transitions to work: masculine identities, youth inequality and labour market change', *Gender, Place and Culture: A Journal of Feminist Geography*, 9(1): 39–59.

McGuiness, F. and Harari, D. (2013) *Work Experience Schemes*, House of Commons Library, Briefing Paper Number 06249, researchbriefings.files.parliament.uk/documents/SN06249/SN06249.pdf

McKee, K. (2009) 'Post-Foucauldian governmentality: what does it offer to critical social policy analysis?', *Critical Social Policy*, 29(3): 465–86.

McKinlay, A. and Starkey, K. (1998) 'Managing Foucault: Foucault, management and organization theory', in McKinlay, A. and Starkey, K. (eds) *Foucault, Management and Organization Theory*, London: Sage Publications, pp. 1–13.

McQuaid, R. and Lindsay, C. (2005) 'The concept of employability', *Urban Studies*, 42(2): 197–219.

McQuaid, R., Green, A. and Danson, M. (2005) 'Introducing employability', *Urban Studies*, 42(2): 191–5.

Meager, N., Bates, P. and Cowling, M. (2003) 'An evaluation of business start-up support for young people', *National Institute Economic Review*, 186(1): 59–72.

Mellors-Bourne, R. and Day, E. (2011) *Evaluation of the Graduate Talent Pool Internships Scheme*, BIS Research Paper Number 28, http://dera.ioe.ac.uk/1814/1/11-668-evaluation-of-graduate-talent-pool-internships.pdf

Mills, M. and Blossfeld, H.P. (2005) 'Globalization, uncertainty and the early life course: a theoretical framework', in H.P. Blossfeld, E. Klijzing, M. Mills, and K. Kurz (eds) *Globalization, Uncertainty and Youth in Society*, New York, NY and Abingdon: Routledge, pp. 1–24.

Mirza-Davies, J. (2015) Youth Contract, Briefing Paper Number 6387, House of Commons Library. http://researchbriefings.files.parliament.uk/documents/SN06387/SN06387.pdf

Mohan, J. and Bulloch, S. (2012) *The Idea of a 'Civic Core': What are the Overlaps between Charitable Giving, Volunteering, and Civic Participation in England and Wales?*, Third Sector Research Centre Working Paper 73, Birmingham: Third Sector Research Centre, University of Birmingham.

Montacute, R. (2018) *Internships–Unpaid, Unadvertised, Unfair*, London: The Sutton Trust.

Mooney, G. and Poole, L. (2004) 'A land of milk and honey? Social policy in Scotland after devolution', *Critical Social Policy*, 24(4): 458–83.

Morgan, A. (2005) 'Governmentality versus choice in contemporary special education', *Critical Social Policy*, 25(3): 325–48.

Morris, P.W.G., Pinto, J.K. and Soderlund, J. (2010) *The Oxford Handbook of Project Management*, Oxford: Oxford University Press.

Mulheirn, I. and Rena, M. (2009) *The Jobs Crisis and What to Do about It*, Social Market Foundation, www.smf.co.uk/publications/the-jobs-crisis-and-what-to-do-about-it

National Audit Office (2007) *Sustainable Employment: Supporting People to Stay in Work and Advance*, www.nao.org.uk/report/sustainable-employment-supporting-people-to-stay-in-work-and-advance

NCVO (National Council for Voluntary Organisations) (2013) *UK Voluntary Sector Workforce Almanac 2013*, London: NCVO.

NELEP (North East Local Enterprise Partnership) (2014) *More and Better Jobs: A Strategic Economic Plan for the North East*, www.nelep.co.uk/wp-content/uploads/2014/11/North-East-Strategic-Economic-Plan-More-and-Better-Jobs.pdf

NELEP (North East Local Enterprise Partnership) Review Team (2013) *The North East LEP Independent Economic Review Summary of the Expert Paper and Evidence Base*. Noth East Local Enterprise Partnership. https://www.nelep.co.uk/wp-content/uploads/2015/02/NE-Economic-Review-Evidence-Base-Summary.pdf

Nenga, S. (2012) 'Not the community, but a community: transforming youth into citizens through volunteer work', *Journal of Youth Studies*, 15(8): 1063–77.

Newton, B., Oakley, J. and Pollard, E. (2011) *Volunteering: Supporting Transitions*, London: NYVS.

Nichols, G. and Ralston, R. (2011) 'Social inclusion through volunteering? The legacy potential of the 2012 Olympic Games', *Sociology*, 45(5): 900–14.

Nicoli, K. and Fejes, A. (2008) 'Mobilizing Foucault in studies of lifelong learning', in A. Fejes and K. Nicoli (eds) *Foucault and Lifelong Learning*, London: Routledge, pp. 1–18.

Nilsen, A. and Brannen, J. (2014) 'An intergenerational approach to transitions to adulthood: the importance of history and biography', *Sociological Research Online*, 19(2): 1–10.

NYA (National Youth Agency) (2015) *Final Report: Commission into Young People and Enterprise*, www.nya.org.uk/wp-content/uploads/2015/01/Commission-into-enterprise-and-young-people-report.pdf

Ockenden, N. and Hill, M. (2009) 'A gateway to work? The role of Volunteer Centres in supporting the link between volunteering and employability', Paper presented at the NCVO/VSSN Researching the Voluntary Sector Conference, Warwick University, 6 September.

O'Connor, H. and Bodicoat, M. (2017) 'Exploitation or opportunity? Student perceptions of internships in enhancing employability skills', *British Journal of Sociology of Education*, 38(4): 435–49.

Olssen, M. and Peters, M.A. (2005) 'Neoliberalism, higher education and the knowledge economy: from the free market to knowledge capitalism', *Journal of Education Policy*, 20(3): 313–45.

Ong, A. (2006) *Neoliberalism as Exception: Mutations in Citizenship and Sovereignty*, Durham, NC: Duke University Press.

Orley, E. (2012) 'Places remember events: towards an ethics of encounter', in H. Andrews and L. Roberts (eds) *Liminal Landscapes: Travel, Experience and Spaces In-Between*, London: Routledge, pp. 36–49.

Orton, M. (2011) 'Flourishing lives: the capabilities approach as a framework for thinking about employment, work and welfare in the 21st century', *Work, Employment and Society*, 25(2): 352–60.

Paisey, C. and Paisey, N. (2010) 'Developing skills via work placements in accounting: student and employer views', *Accounting Forum*, 34(2): 89–108.

Peck, J. and Theodore, N. (2000) 'Beyond "employability"', *Cambridge Journal of Economics*, 24: 729–49.

Peck, J. and Theodore, N. (2001) 'Exporting workfare/importing welfare-to-work: exploring the politics of third way policy transfer', *Political Geography*, 20: 427–60.

Pegg, A. and Caddell, M. (2016) 'Workplaces and policy spaces: insights from third sector internships Scotland', *Higher Education Skills and Work-Based Learning*, 6(2): 162–77.

Perlin, R. (2011) *Intern Nation: How to Earn Nothing and Learn Little in the Brave New Economy*, London: Verso.

Price, R., McDonald, P., Bailey, J. and Pini, B. (2011) *Young People and Work*, Farnham, Ashgate.

Prior, D. and Barnes, M. (2011) 'Subverting social policy on the front line: agencies of resistance in the delivery of services', *Social Policy and Administration*, 45(3): 264–79.

Putnam, R. (2000) *Bowling Alone: The Collapse and Revival of American Society*, New York, NY: Simon & Schuster.

Quintin, G. and Martin, S. (2014) *Same but Different: School-to-Work Transitions in Emerging and Advanced Economies*, OECD Social, Employment and Migration Papers No. 154, Paris: OECD Publishing.

Roberman, S. (2014) 'Labour activation policies and the seriousness of simulated work', *Social Anthropology*, 22(3): 326–39.

Roberts, S. (2011) 'Beyond "NEET" and "tidy" pathways: considering the "missing middle" of youth transition studies', *Journal of Youth Studies*, 14(1): 21–39.

Roberts, S. (2012) 'One step forward, one step back: a contribution to the ongoing conceptual debate in youth studies', *Journal of Youth Studies*, 15(3): 389–401.

Roberts, S. and Evans, S. (2013) 'Aspirations and imagined futures: the im/possibilities for Britain's young working class', in W. Atkinson, S. Roberts and M. Savage (eds) *Class Inequality in Austerity Britain*, Basingstoke: Palgrave Macmillan, pp. 70–89.

Roberts, S. and MacDonald, R. (2013) 'Introduction for Special Section of Sociological Research Online. The marginalised mainstream: making sense of the "missing middle" of youth studies', *Sociological Research Online*, 18(1).

Rochester, C., Ellis-Paine, A. and Howlett, S. (2010) *Volunteering and Society in the 21st Century*, Basingstoke: Palgrave Macmillan.

Rose, N. (1999) *Governing the Soul: Shaping of the Private Self*, London: Routledge.

Russell Commission (2005) *A National Framework for Youth Action and Engagement*, https://webarchive.nationalarchives.gov.uk/20060214050033/http://www.russellcommission.org/docs/Executive_summary.pdf

Russell, L., Simmons, R. and Thompson, R. (2011) 'Ordinary lives: an ethnographic study of young people attending entry to employment programmes', *Journal of Education and Work*, 24(5): 477–99.

Sarasvathy, S.D. (2008) 'What makes entrepreneurs entrepreneurial?', SSRN, https://papers.ssrn.com/abstract=909038

Shade, I. and Jacobson, J. (2015) 'Hungry for the job: gender, unpaid internships and the creative industries', *The Sociological Review*, 63(1): 188–205.

Shaw, J. and MacKinnon, D. (2011) 'Moving on with "filling in"? Some thoughts on state restructuring after devolution', *Area*, 43, 23–30.

Shildrick, T., Blackman, S. and MacDonald, R. (2009) 'Young people, class and place', *Journal of Youth Studies*, 12(5): 457–65.

Schoon, I. (2014) 'Parental worklessness and the experience of NEET among their offspring', *Longitudinal and Life Course Studies*, 5: 129–50.

Shutt, J. and Sutherland, J. (2003) 'Encouraging the transition into self-employment', *Regional Studies*, 37(1): 97–103.

Siebert, S. and Wilson, F. (2013) 'All work and no pay: consequences of unpaid work in the creative industries', *Work, Employment and Society*, 27(4): 711–21.

Simmons, R. (2017) 'Employability, knowledge and the creative arts: reflections from an ethnographic study of NEET young people on an entry to employment programme', *Research in Post-Compulsory Education*, 22(1): 22–37.

Simmons, R., Russell, L. and Thomson, R. (2014a) 'Young people and labour market marginality: findings from a longitudinal ethnographic study', *Journal of Youth Studies*, 17(5): 577–91.

Simmons, R., Thomson, R. and Russell, L. (2014b) *Education, Work and Social Change: Young People and Marginalization in Post-Industrial Britain*, Basingstoke: Palgrave Macmillan.

Smith, R. (2014) *The Gorbals and Oatlands: A New History. Volume 1: The Gorbals of Old*, Catrine: Stenlake Publishing.

Smith, R., Bell, R. and Watts, H. (2014) 'Personality trait differences between traditional and social entrepreneurs', *Social Enterprise Journal*, 10(3): 200–21.

Social Mobility and Child Poverty Commission (2014) *State of the Nation 2014: Social Mobility and Child Poverty in Great Britain*, https://assets.publishing.service.gov.uk/government/uploads/system/uploads/attachment_data/file/365765/State_of_Nation_2014_Main_Report.pdf

Spielhofer, T., Golden, S. and Evans, K. (2011) *Young People's Aspirations in Rural Areas*, Slough: National Foundation for Educational Research.

Spyridakis, M. (2013) *The Liminal Worker*, Farnham: Ashgate.

Standing, G. (2011) *The Precariat: The New Dangerous Class*, London: Bloomsbury.

Sunley, P., Martin, R. and Nativel, C. (2001) 'Mapping the New Deal: local disparities in the performance of welfare-to-work', *Transactions of the Institute of British Geographers*, 26(4): 484–512.

Tholen, G. (2013) *We Need to Talk about Graduates: The Changing Nature of the UK Graduate Labour Market*, SKOPE Monograph No. 15, Oxford: SKOPE, Department of Education, University of Oxford.

Thomassen, B. (2012) 'Revisiting liminality: the danger of empty spaces', in H. Andrews, and L. Roberts (eds) *Liminal Landscapes: Travel, Experience and Spaces In-Between*, London: Routledge, pp. 21–35.

Thompson, J. (2011) 'A comparative empirical analysis of characteristics associated with accounting internships', *International Journal of Business, Humanities and Technology*, 1(1): 54.

Thomson, R. (2011) 'Individualisation and social exclusion: the case of young people not in education, employment or training', *Oxford Review of Education*, 37(6): 785–802.

Thomson, P. and Russell, L. (2009) 'Data, data everywhere – but not all the numbers that count? Mapping alternative provisions for students excluded from school', *International Journal of Inclusive Education*, 13(4): 423–438.

Tomaszewski, W. and Cebulla, A. (2014) 'Jumping off the track: comparing the experiences of first jobs of young people living in disadvantaged and non-disadvantaged neighbourhoods in Britain', *Journal of Youth Studies*, 17(8): 1029–45.

Tomlinson, M. (2007) 'Graduate employability and student attitudes and orientations to the labour market', *Journal of Education and Work*, 20(4): 285–304.

Tomlinson, S. (2013) *Ignorant Yobs? Low Attainers in a Global Knowledge Economy*, London: Routledge.

TUC (Trades Union Congress) (2014) *Youth Unemployment and Ethnicity*, www.tuc.org.uk/sites/default/files/BMEyouthunemployment.pdf

TUC (2016) 'BAME workers with degrees two and half times more likely to be unemployed', www.tuc.org.uk/news/bame-workers-degrees-two-and-half-times-more-likely-be-unemployed-finds-tuc

Turner, V. (1974) *Dramas, Fields and Metaphors: Symbolic Action in Human Society*, Ithaca, NY: Cornell University Press.

UKCES (UK Commission for Employment and Skills) (2013) *Scaling the Youth Employment Challenge*, https://assets.publishing.service.gov.uk/government/uploads/system/uploads/attachment_data/file/305806/scaling-the-youth-employment-challenge-report.pdf

UK Government (nd) *Budget 2018*, www.gov.uk/government/publications/budget-2018-documents/budget-2018

Universities UK (2002) *Enhancing Employability, Recognising Diversity: Making Links Between Higher Education and the World of Work*, www.qualityresearchinternational.com/Harvey%20papers/Harvey,%20Locke%20and%20Morey%202002%20Enhancing%20employability.pdf

Urciuoli, B. (2008) 'Skills and selves in the new workplace', *American Ethnologist*, 35(2): 211–28.

Van Gennep, A. (1960) *The Rites of Passage*, London: Routledge.

Wade, J. and Dixon, J. (2006) 'Making a home, finding a job: investigating early housing and employment outcomes for young people leaving care', *Child and Family Social Work*, 11(3): 199–208.

Walker, P. (2013) 'Unpaid interns: 100 firms being investigated by HMRC', *The Guardian*, 12 April, www.theguardian.com/uk/2013/apr/12/unpaid-interns-100-firms-investigated

Walkerdine, V., Lucey, H. and Melody, J. (2001) *Growing Up Girl: Psycho-Social Explorations of Gender and Class*, London: Palgrave.

Warburton, J. and Smith, J. (2003) 'Out of the generosity of your heart: are we creating active citizens through compulsory volunteer programmes for young people in Australia?', *Social Policy and Administration*, 37(7): 772–86.

Waring, J. and Brierton, J. (2011) 'Women's enterprise and the Scottish economy', *International Journal of Gender and Entrepreneurship*, 3(2): 144–63.

White, J. (2017) *Urban Music and Entrepreneurship: Beats, Rhymes and Young People's Enterprise*, *Routledge Advances in Sociology*, Abingdon: Routledge.

White, R. and Green, A. (2011) 'Opening up or closing down opportunities? The role of social networks and attachment to place in informing young peoples' attitudes and access to training and employment', *Urban Studies*, 48(1): 41–60.

Wilde, R.J. (2016) ' "Plugging gaps, taking action": conceptions of global citizenship in gap year volunteering', *Policy and Practice: A Development Education Review*, 23: 65–85.

Wilde, R.J. and Leonard, P. (2018) 'Youth enterprise: the role of gender and life stage in motivations, aspirations and measures of success', *Journal of Education and Work*, 31(2): 144–58.

Wilson, J. (2000) 'Volunteering', *Annual Review of Sociology*, 26: 215–40.

Wilson, T. (2014) *A Review of Business–University Collaboration*, Department of Business, Innovation and Skills, https://assets. publishing.service.gov.uk/government/uploads/system/uploads/ attachment_data/file/32383/12-610-wilson-review-business-university-collaboration.pdf

Wilton, N. (2011) 'Do employability skills really matter in the UK labour market? The case of business and management graduates', *Work, Employment Society*, 25(1): 85–100.

Woolvin, M., Mills, S., Hardill, I. and Rutherford, A. (2015) 'Divergent geographies of policy and practice? Voluntarism and devolution in England, Scotland and Wales', *The Geographical Journal*, 181(1): 38–46.

Work Foundation (2014) *Research Highlights Youth Unemployment 'Blackspots'*, https://www.bmgresearch.co.uk/research-highlights-youth-unemployment-blackspots

Worth, S. (2005) 'Beating the "churning" trap in the youth labour market', *Work, Employment and Society*, 19(2): 403–14.

Young, Lord (2014) *Enterprise for All: The Relevance of Enterprise in Education*, www.gov.uk/government/uploads/system/uploads/ attachment_data/file/338749/EnterpriseforAll-lowres-200614.pdf

Index

A

accountancy firms *see* internships
Action Plan: The European Agenda
　for Entrepreneurship 57–8
'active citizenship',
　volunteering as 113
Adonis, Andrew 37
adult learning 17
apprenticeships 6
Asian ethnic groups, work and
　employment patterns 14

B

Barnes, M. 19
Baudrillard, J. 81
Bauman, Z. 156
Baxter, J. 16
Beck, U. 81, 88, 154, 156
Beck-Gernsheim, E. 88
benefit sanctions 10
'betrayed generation' 11
'Big Four' accountancy firms *see*
　internships
Big Lottery funding 116
Black ethnic groups, work and
　employment patterns 14
Blackburn, R.A. 59, 74
Blatterer, H. 11, 150
'blue-chip' companies *see* internships
'brand ambassadors,' interns as 94–5
BTSD (Bridging the Skills Divide)
　programme 41–54
　see also North East, employability
　case study

C

Cameron, David 61–2
'career management' 32
Cartmel, F. 81, 154
Chinese students, and internships
　104, 106–7

Citizen Education Longitudinal
　Survey dataset 117
City and Guilds accreditation, North
　East employability case study
　25, 42, 50
coalition government
　enterprise policies 61–2
　internship policies 89
　youth employment policies 35
Colvin, G. 156
Commonwealth Games 2014,
　Glasgow 22, 117–18, 120, 136, 144
Community Action
　programme, UK 34
Community Programme, UK 34
conditionality 10
Conservative governments, enterprise
　policies 62–3
Conservative Party, unpaid
　internships 91
Cridland, John 1
Crisp, R. 7–8
Crossley, L. 1
Curran, J. 59, 74

D

Davis Smith, J. 113
Dean, J. 15, 17
Deetz, S. 56, 73, 77
deindustrialization 4–5, 31
　Glasgow 21, 151–2
　North East 21, 144–5, 151–2
demand-side factors in
　employability 10
　see also supply side factors in
　employability
Department for Work and Pensions
　see DWP (Department for Work
　and Pensions)
'dependency culture' 61
de-traditionalism 11
digital economy 156
　North East 37

disability, young people with, work and employment patterns 14
disciplinary form of power-knowledge 16–17
discourse analysis 17–18
discursive field, in post-Foucauldian governmentality approach 3, 15
diversity, lack of in elite professional service firms 95–6
DWP (Department for Work and Pensions)
    Move into Work Scheme 119–20
    Volunteer Brokerage Scheme 114, 115–16
    Work Together scheme 114, 116

E

Economic and Social Research Council (ESRC) 2, 20
economic recession (2008–12) 1, 8, 9, 11, 12
    EU youth unemployment policy 33
    and internships 83, 84–5
    and volunteering 111
    and youth unemployment 1, 5–6, 33, 61, 113–14, 117
education system, UK
    inequality of outcomes in 8
    perceived deficits in 6–7
Ellis Paine, A. 117
employability 2, 3, 29–30
    BTSD (Bridging the Skills Divide) programme 41–54
    as a concept 9–10, 29
    definition of 30
    demand-side factors in 10
    discourses of 7, 24–5, 30–2, 53–4
    and liminality 149–54
    and neoliberalism 20, 29
    North East case study 2, 21, 22–3, 24–5, 29–30, 36–41, 52–4, 141, 144–5, 146–7, 151–2, 154–5
    policies and market interventions 33–6
    and regionality 142, 143–6
    supply-side factors in 10, 31, 54

'supply-side fundamentalism' 9–10
    and TSOs (third sector organizations) 8–9
    Volunteering Makes Sense programme 120–38
    Volunteer Centres 116–17
    and the 'workfare state' 18
employers
    crucial role in youth employability 10
    North East employability case study 42–3
    see also internships
Employment Action programme, UK 34
enterprise 9
    discourses of 57–60
    EU (European Union) policies 57–8, 60, 62
    and gender 59
    'mindset' for 57, 58, 59, 60, 61
    and neoliberalism 57, 81
    policy context 60–3
    risk and failure 26, 55, 58, 60, 63, 75, 77, 78
    South Coast case study 2, 21, 22, 23, 25–6, 55–6, 63–6, 80–2, 141, 147–8, 152, 155–6
    EY (Enterprising Youth) programme 55, 56, 73–80, 81–2, 147, 155–6
    SEU Enterprise Bootcamp 55, 56, 66–73, 72, 75, 80–1, 80–2, 147, 155–6
    young people's motivations for 59
Enterprise Champions 61
Enterprising Youth 65
Entry to Employment programme, UK 7
ESRC (Economic and Social Research Council) 2, 20
EU (European Union)
    funding for TVC, Glasgow 120
    loss of funding after UK withdrawal 40
    migrants to UK 43
    youth employment policies 7, 33
European 2020 Growth Strategy 33

European Employment Strategy 31, 33
European Social Fund 22, 33
EY (Enterprising Youth) programme, South Coast enterprise case study 55, 56, 73–80, 81–2, 147, 155–6

F

failure, and enterprise 26, 55, 60, 75, 77
  see also risk
flexible employment 32
football club internship 104–6
Foucault, M. 14–15, 25, 26, 51, 73, 77, 81, 131, 133
  on power 16–17
  technologies 55–6
  see also post-Foucauldian governmentality approach
France, A. 149
freelance work *see* enterprise
Furlong, A. 6, 81, 154
Further and Higher Education Act 1992 66n1
further education institutions, and Youth Opportunities Programme 7
Future Jobs Fund, UK 34

G

Garsten, C. 152
Gateshead 43, 52
  see also North East, employability case study
gender:
  and enterprise 59
  and internships 96
  structural inequalities 12
  work and employment patterns 13–14
gentrification, in Glasgow 128–9
'getting in' and 'getting on' 32
Giddens, A. 154, 156
Glasgow
  Commonwealth Games 2014 22, 117–18, 120, 136, 144
  deindustrialization and structural decline 21, 151–2
  funding 22

volunteering case study 2, 21, 22–3, 26–7, 111–12, 117–20, 141, 142, 144, 148–9, 151–2, 153, 154–5
  VMS (Volunteering Makes Sense) project 27, 120–38
Glasgow City Council 117, 118, 119, 120
Global Entrepreneurship Week 61
Glucksmann, M. 143
governmentality 14–15, 17, 18–19, 26, 55–6, 81, 133
  see also post-Foucauldian governmentality approach
Graduate Talent Pool Internships 114
'graduate trainee schemes' 88
graduates
  Black and Asian 14
  impact of 2008–12 economic recession on 13
  racial inequalities in work and employment patterns 14
  see also university students
'Great Recession' 5, 11
  see also economic recession (2008–12)
Greene, F.J. 63
Griffiths, Andrew 91
guanxi 104, 106
Guile, D. 87

H

'hands-off' culture 84, 89
hard-to-reach groups 153–4
  see also NEETS
Hartlepool 43, 46–51, 146–7
  see also North East, employability case study

I

ILO (International Labour Organization) 5
individualization 11, 18, 57, 88, 127, 140–1, 154
Industrial Strategy, UK 62
inequality *see* social inequality
Institute for Public Policy Research 92
internships 9, 83–4, 108–9

bifurcated discourse of 84–9
London case study 2, 21–2, 23, 26, 84, 92–3, 93–109, 141, 145, 148, 151, 155
and neoliberalism 88, 98–100
policy context 89–93, 114
and social class 83–4, 86, 88–9, 95–7, 108–9
unpaid 86, 90–2, 104
interventionist practices, in post-Foucauldian governmentality approach 15
interview training, North East employability case study 42, 45–6

J

Javid, Sajid 62
'jilted generation' 8, 11
Jobcentre Plus 24, 117, 119, 120
Jobs in Business Glasgow 120
JSA (Job Seekers Allowance) 34, 35
Work Experience Scheme 114

K

knowledge-based industries, transition to 5, 31

L

Labour government
Future Jobs Fund 34
New Deal policy 31, 34, 61
'Third Way' policies 31
Lahiff, A. 87
Lawton, K. 87
Lee, D. 83
LEP (Local Enterprise Partnership)
enterprise schemes on the South Coast case study 23, 65–6
NELEP (North East LEP) 37, 38, 40, 65, 147
Levebvre, H. 20
life stage, and enterprise 59
lifelong learning 32
liminality 142, 149–54
cultural 150–1, 152
economic 150–1, 152–3

physical 150, 152–2
temporal 150
Lindsay, C. 31, 53
Lippard, L. 151
liquid modernity 11
LLAKES Centre for Research on Learning and Life Chances 2, 20
Local Enterprise Partnership see LEP (Local Enterprise Partnership)
London
internships case study 2, 21–2, 23, 26, 84, 92–3, 93–109, 141, 145, 148, 151, 155
youth unemployment 21–2
London Youth 40
'lost generation' 5
Lyotard, J.-F. 81

M

MacDonald, R. 61
macro-level (national) analysis 19
'Mandatory Work Activity,' UK 35
Massey, D. 143
May, Theresa 62–3
McKee, K. 14, 18–19
McQuaid, R. 31, 53
Meager, N. 59
meso-level (regional) analysis 19
micro-level (organizational) analysis 3, 19
middle classes 6, 13
and internships 84, 88–9, 95–7, 108, 148
see also social class
migrants
North East 43
VMS (Volunteering Makes Sense) programme, Glasgow 121
'mindset,' for enterprise 57, 58, 59, 60, 61
'missing middle' 13
North East 39–40, 44
mobility issues in employment
North East 39, 52, 53
motivation, North East employability case study 44

Move into Work Scheme
(DWP) 119–20

N

National Citizen Service 114
National Young Volunteers
Service 114
NEETS (young people not in
education, employment or training)
and coalition government youth
employment policies, UK 35
EU youth employment policies 33
'hidden NEETS' 40, 44
North East 38, 44
NELEP (North East Local Enterprise
Partnership) 37, 38, 40, 65, 147
neoliberalism 11, 140–1
and employability 20, 29
and enterprise 57, 81
and internships 88, 98–100
and Volunteering Makes Sense
programme 123
and welfare policies 116
New Deal for Young People
programme, UK 34
New Deal policy, UK 31, 34, 61
New Labour government *see* Labour
government
'no-rescue' culture 84, 89, 109
North East
deindustrialization and structural
decline 21, 144–5, 151–2
employability case study 2, 21,
22–3, 24–5, 29–30, 36–41,
52–4, 141, 144–5, 146–7,
151–2, 154–5
BTSD (Bridging the Skills Divide)
programme 41–54
regional economic context 36–41
youth unemployment levels 21

O

OGO (Office for Graduate
Opportunities) 89
Organisation for Economic
Co-operation and
Development 31

Orley, E. 151
over-50 age group, North
East 38

P

Panel on Fair Access to the
Professions 86
Peck, J. 9–10
place 141
regionality and employability
142, 143–6
post-Foucauldian governmentality
approach 3, 15–16, 20, 139–40
post-modernism 81
poststructuralism 16
Potter, D. 87
Powell, R. 7–8
power 16
Foucault's analysis of 15, 16–17
'precariat' 5
precarious employment 32
Prior, D. 19

R

race
and internships 96
structural inequalities 12
work and employment patterns 14
regeneration 128–9, 144
regionality 142, 143–6
research outline 20–3
responsibilization 18, 57, 81, 88, 113,
127, 140–1, 156
risk 12, 142, 154–6
and enterprise 26, 55, 58, 60, 63,
75, 77, 78
'risk society' 81, 154
Roberts, S. 13, 149
Rose, N. 16
Russell Commission 113
Russell Group universities 66
Russell, L. 52

S

Sarasvathy, S.D. 72
Scottish Employability Award 122

Scottish Government 23, 117, 118–19, 120
security form of power-knowledge 16–17
self-employment *see* enterprise
self-governance 16, 18, 25, 30, 51, 131–2
and internships 88, 91
self-improvement 16
service sector
North East 37
transition to 5
SEU Enterprise Bootcamp, South Coast enterprise case study 55, 56, 66–73, 72, 75, 80–1, 80–2, 147, 155–6
skills deficits in young people 6–8
Skills Development Scotland 117, 120
small businesses 57
see also enterprise
social class 146, 154
and internships 83–4, 86, 88–9, 95–7, 108–9
as research focus 21–2
and social inequality 2–3, 12–13
social inequality 142, 146–9
in education outcomes 8
and social class 2–3, 12–13
social mobility 8, 149
Social Mobility Commission 86
South Coast
enterprise case study 2, 21, 22, 23, 25–6, 55–6, 63–6, 80–2, 141, 147–8, 152, 155–6
EY (Enterprising Youth) programme 55, 56, 73–80, 81–2, 147, 155–6
SEU Enterprise Bootcamp 55, 56, 66–73, 72, 75, 80–1, 80–2, 147, 155–6
youth unemployment 21, 22
sovereign form of power-knowledge 16–17
space
and liminality 150
see also place
spending cuts 10

Storey, D.J. 63
student gap years 17
'subject, the,' in poststructuralism 16
supply-side factors in employability 10, 31, 54
'supply-side fundamentalism' 9–10

T

technologies of production, sign systems, power and the self (Foucault) 55–6
TG (Tenement Gardens), Glasgow 127–9, 132–3
Theodore, N. 9–10
'Third Way' policies, Labour government 31
transitions 45, 11–14, 108–9, 123
TSOs (third sector organizations), and employability training 8–9, 116
Turner, V. 150
TVC (The Volunteer Centre), Glasgow 120–38, 137

U

unemployment case management 17
United Nations 31
universities
North East 38–9
Russell Group 66
see also SEU Enterprise Bootcamp, South Coast enterprise case study
unpaid work 114–15
internships 86, 90–2, 104
see also volunteering
Unpaid Work Prohibition Bill 86

V

Van Gennep, A. 150
VBS (Volunteer Brokerage Scheme), (DWP) 114, 115–16
vinvolved (National Young Volunteers Service) 114
VMS (Volunteering Makes Sense) programme, Glasgow 27, 120–38
vocational competency-based training 17

vocational education and training
  gender patterns in 14
Volunteer Brokerage Scheme (VBS),
  (DWP) 114, 115–16
Volunteer Centre, The (TVC),
  Glasgow 120–38, 137
Volunteer Centres 115–16
volunteering 17, 27, 111–12, 136–8
  'active citizenship' 113
  definition of 113
  discourses of 112–15
  Glasgow, case study 2, 21, 22–3,
    26–7, 111–12, 117–20, 141, 142,
    144, 148–9, 151–2, 153, 154–5
  VMS (Volunteering Makes Sense)
    project 120–38
  policy context 115–17
  as work experience 9
Volunteering for Stronger
  Communities project 116

W

'welfare dependency' 8
welfare policies 116
  harshening climate of 10
  and neoliberalism 116
Wilson review 85
women
  work and employment
    patterns 13–14
  see also gender
work experience 9, 114–15
  Move into Work Scheme 119–20

North East, employability case study
  42–3, 44–5
university students 85
VMS programme 127–36, 137–8
  see also internships; volunteering
Work Experience Scheme for Job
  Seekers Allowance 114
Work Programme, UK 7, 35–6
Work Together scheme (DWP)
  114, 116
'workfare state' 18
working classes 6, 13
  and internships 84, 89
  see also social class
'worklessness' 7

Y

young carers 14
Young Person's Guarantee, UK 7
Youth Contract, UK 35, 61
Youth Employment Initiative 33
Youth Guarantee (EU) 7, 33
youth non-participation 17
Youth Opportunities
  Programme, UK 7
youth unemployment 21,
  117–18, 136
  2008–12 economic recession 1,
    5–6, 33, 61, 113–14, 117
youth-to-work transitions
  'extended' or 'delayed' 12
  global and national context 4–14
YVNE (Youth View North East)
  41–54, 146, 147